Vamps
Don't Sleep Alone

Vampires Don't Sleep Alone

Your Guide to Meeting,
Dating and Seducing a Vampire

ELIZABETH BARRIAL
AND D.H. ALTAIR

Ulysses Press

Published in the United States by
Ulysses Press
P.O. Box 3440
Berkeley, CA 94703
www.ulyssespress.com

ISBN 978-1-56975-785-7
Library of Congress Control Number 2009943780

Acquisitions Editor: Keith Riegert
Managing Editor: Claire Chun
Editorial & production: Lauren Harrison, Judith Metzener
Cover design: what!design @ whatweb.com
Cover illustration: © istockphoto.com/Larysa Dodz

Printed in the United States by Bang Printing

10 9 8 7 6 5 4 3 2 1

Distributed by Publishers Group West

For my writing partner, whose kindness, wit,
and wisdom buoys me.
For my beloved brother, my beautiful husband,
and Lilith, our dhampyr.
My life is ashes without you.
For my family, blood and non-blood, living and dead.
With all my heart, I love you.
Sine amore, nihil est vita.
Elizabeth Barrial

For Lilith (Grandpa's sidekick)—
When you look back treat me kindly;
and to Lisa Majewski—It's only make-believe.
D. H. Altair

Contents

Introduction

The Art of Love: knowing how to combine the temperament of a vampire with the discretion of an anemone.—E. M. Cioran

It is a summer night, and the full moon provides plenty of light as you head to the club. The light mist in the air and the cool dampness feel good against your exposed skin. You have done your make-up to perfection and are wearing your sexiest dress, the one that fits your body like a silk glove and accentuates all of your assets. The tops of your breasts are dusted with glitter. Your lips are red, a deep, blood red, and your smoky eyes beg men to come to you, to need you, to desire you. But you are only after one man tonight. This is a man who can be as dark as the night and as stoic as the grave. This man can offer you eternal love.

You had planned on a Friday night at home so you could finish up some paperwork. Long hours sitting at a desk, staring at a computer monitor, have left you feeling tense and claustrophobic, so you decide to go for a walk to unwind before you hit the sack. Stepping out into the cool

darkness, you look up at the harvest moon, hanging low, full, and darkly golden in the sky. The reflective light from the orb casts long, dark shadows across the ground, creating shapes that shift and slide as you walk past. The sounds of the night come to you—a train in the distance, a cat in the alley, and a…well, you are not quite sure what that is—and you move on.

It is dark inside the nightclub, and the gloom is punctuated by jagged slashes of multicolored laser light and staccato flashes from the strobes. The air is damp and uncomfortably warm from the heat of writhing, dancing bodies, and the air is thick with tobacco, clove, heady perfume, and spilled gin. As you make your way through the crowd, you feel your own heartbeat throb in your throat, and your pulse races in anticipation of tonight's events. You can feel moisture slowly trickle down between your swollen breasts as your breathing quickens. You know you look enticing. Your hair ruffles a moment as you pass a fan, and you are quick to straighten it with a couple of swift moves of your fingers. You want to look your best because tonight is the night. Tonight you are planning on meeting your vampire. The Transylvanian nobleman to your fair and seductive Lucy awaits, and you are ready for the chance at eternal romance.

Being alone has its advantages: It gives you time to think. You have been working day and night, and your work is your life; it always has been, but not by choice. You have always been something of a loner, introverted, and though you have had many girlfriends, you haven't yet found anyone who really understands you. In all of your relationships, you have felt a desolate aloneness. Despite your many liaisons, you have not been able to find a real connection. You are looking for something more than the women you have met have been able to offer you. Unlike most of your buddies, you are looking for something serious, something lasting. You are looking for a love that is transcendent, the stuff of poetry, and not the shallow banalities that your peers seem to relish. Her eyes will be pools deep into her soul, and she will know all your needs and yearnings from the moment you meet her. She is out there, and you know it. You can feel it. But where do you find this sort of passion and romance in a world of glass, steel, and diodes? Where do you find the key to eternity?

While the ultraviolet darkness of the club surrounds you in a cape of pounding musical beats, people bump you as they pass, and you check out their faces and scan the crowd for this vampire of your dreams. He is there. You know this as well as you know your own name. Your pulse quickens. You imagine his breath on your neck and the warmth of your own blood as it pounds through your heart, bringing in the oxygen. It is as red as it can get, and you are a ripe piece of vampiric fruit. You can imagine his hand wrapping itself around your neck and then flattening out as his fingers trail down toward your breasts. You know it is time, and you think you are ready.

She is your succubus, your vampire. Her heat is palpable as you imagine her floating down to you or stepping around the corner of that hedge up ahead. You would do anything to meet her. You would sell your soul.

BUT WAIT! WHAT THE HECK ARE YOU DOING?

If you are seeking romance in the arms of a vampire, you need to read this book. Information is strength. You need to arm yourself with knowledge about what you are getting into. You need help. Because of the fairly recent assimilation of vampires into human society, more and more humans are taking up these complex relationships, making access to this information vital, now more than ever. In this book, we present a brief history of the vampire and some theories of vampire sociology. We discuss common misconceptions of these long-maligned and often misunderstood creatures and how to responsibly form relationships, romantic and otherwise, with them.

When you have finished reading this book, you may still want to spend eternity with your vampire. We hope that at least we may help you to pick the right vampire for you, and we want to enable you to go into this relationship with your eyes open, armed with information, knowing exactly what you are getting yourself into. This knowledge comes from years of study and our own personal infiltration of the vampire culture. It's secret information available only to those who are part of the inner circle. Come in. Just don't tell anybody that we told you these things.

Part One

Your Introduction to Vampires:

What You Need to Know

Why a Vampire?

The nosferatu do not die like the bee when he stings once.
He is only stronger; and being stronger,
have yet more power to work evil.
—Abraham Van Helsing, *Dracula*

The old Greek term *nosophoros* means "plague carrier," and vampires and assorted drinkers of blood have always been associated with carrying and spreading disease. This is hardly the most attractive premise on which to go out and find a date, mate, or even acquaintance. An odd place for us to begin, don't you agree? But do not delude yourself. Your quest to conquer your vampire lover will not happen without prejudices and dissent from not only the mere mortals around you but other vampires and their lovers as well. What makes these denizens of darkness so appealing? What do they have to offer that seems so out of reach by any other means?

The vampiric condition has existed since the beginning of recorded history, and the mysteries of

17

it have been mythologized by many cultures as a way of understanding the blood-drinkers among us. Vampires' dietary habits, lifestyles, and appearances lend easily to creating anxiety among humanity's general population. The Pishacha and Vetelas of India, the Greco-Roman Empusae and Lamia, the Babylonian Gallû—all these mythological figures were exaggerated, deliberately misleading accounts of the vampire, based on a self-perpetuating cycle of bad publicity rooted in humanity's fear of the unknown. In traditional Western folklore, vampires have often been portrayed as reanimated corpses with tight skin from bloating and long dirty fingernails due to receding of the skin from the cuticles down, which caused the nails to appear as if their growth had continued unimpeded after death. These rotting, stinking, semi-decayed undead would never do as romantic partners. In truth, many of history's great statesmen, religious leaders, scientists, and artists were vampires forced to mimic humanity in order to survive, though this information is the type of stuff you will never find in your school history books.

Now, in the twenty-first century, we are beginning to put aside superstitious, foolish fears and embrace vampires as our friends and lovers. The modern acceptance of the vampiric condition is owed in part, ironically, to the popularity of Bram Stoker's 1897 novel *Dracula*. Though the antagonist is portrayed as a monster, and the vampires that populate the story are depicted as little more than predators, the sexuality, worldliness, and mystery of Stoker's story led many free-thinking individuals in the late Victorian era to actively seek out vampires in society, which, as a consequence, brought us to the acceptance of vampires that we are starting to enjoy today. The vampire has been gussied up, and both his attire and appearance have become more socially acceptable.

A relationship with a vampire is not without its challenges, but it can be an incomparably fulfilling experience for a human. Where we need to start and concentrate our focus is the modern vampire, the man you are destined to seek out and spend eternity with, the man who will literally sweep you off of you feet and into a mausoleum built for two. Let us bring him up to date.

In the eighteenth and nineteenth centuries, the quintessential vision of the vampire changed from that earlier, folkloric image. In literary representations, the vampire was now portrayed as romantic, cultured royalty, dapper in formal attire—a rake or vixen in the gilded guise of aristocracy—thanks to the writings of Bram Stoker, Joseph Sheridan Le Fanu, John Polidori, and Alexandre Dumas. By the twentieth century, the image of the vampire was that of a darkly beautiful, hip, sensual, and dangerous *puer aeternus*, his image molded by the writings of Anne Rice, Poppy Z. Brite, Charlaine Harris, and Chelsea Quinn Yarbro. Though the fantasy of a vampiric liaison was a dangerous one, the promise of never-ending romance and indescribable passion remained ubiquitous. Now, the allegorical vamp was ready for general socialization, a motion picture career, and prime-time television. The media portrayal of the vampire is brimming with unbridled, feral sexuality, romantic mystery, and the promise of undying devotion. Is it any wonder that humans feel drawn to this?

But despite the erotic allure, why date a vampire? What would motivate a person to deliberately choose, with open eyes, to face the inevitable challenges in this uniquely complex, exigent type of relationship?

Thanks to their innumerable years on earth, vampires have acquired a self-confidence and worldliness that is impossible for humans to achieve. Often, vampires also tend to have more refined tastes, and their manners are generally impeccable. Occasionally, their cultural references may be somewhat dated and their choice of words archaic, but it is a small price of inconvenience compared with the pleasure of sharing the breadth of their centuries of experience in all knowledge and pleasures:

- Vampires are almost wholly immune to illness and do not age.
- The vampire, male or female, is a fountainhead of passion. It is a literal byproduct of the condition and is biologically fueled by the engorgement of the red blood cells in the vampire's system. The result? They have unparalleled primal sexual

energy and, as a consequence of their extensive time on earth, prowess and skill unmatched in humans.

All in all, there is no substitute for the very rich, and sometimes enjoyable, experience of being a vampire's consort.

Tortured Soul: It Comes with the Territory

Such are the autumn people. Beware of them.
—Ray Bradbury, *Something Wicked This Way Comes*

It has become a cliché of sorts, thanks to nineteenth and twentieth century vampire fiction, that vampires are universally possessed of tragic, tortured souls, and that they can find a sort of redemption through romance. But it is a cliché that has some foundation in truth. No, not all vampires are larger-than-life Byronic antiheroes, but many are. The life of a vampire is an inexplicably lonely one, and it would be fair to say that he is doomed to this loneliness by his very nature.

The vampire's extended lifespan is something that many people find enviable. Death is not something that modern Western culture finds palatable. Long gone are the days when we employed wailing women, celebrated death through creating memorial jewelry of hair and jet, or practiced postmortem photography. We simply no longer truly celebrate death through elaborate memorials; death is something to be feared, and is only spoken of in hushed whispers, lest the reaper come calling. As a result, the vastly extended lifespan of the vampire is something that modern humans covet. But is eternal life something that we really want for ourselves?

My God! Can one truly imagine the agony of living forever? The initial idea is great: You will never die and, with a little luck, will always appear healthy and strong. A few limitations will come up here and there, but overall it's just life, life, and more life. But as someone who is about to date and, hopefully, mate with a vampire for life, you have to ask, What is eternity and what problems and blessings come with it? Most humans have a hard time putting together five years of bliss, let alone forever.

Consider the sorrow that comes from watching the eons pass. It would be impossible for a vampire to confer the vampiric pathogen to all the people he or she loved in their human lifetime. (Whoa, we just got a whiff of Mormon vampirisim—talk about an extended family!) Watching all the people they love wither and die while they stay eternally vibrant and strong is painful, to say the least. Vampires are also met with the challenge of watching all that is familiar to them erode, change, and be rebuilt. They must find ways to acclimate and adapt to societal change and upheaval, often watching whole systems of behavior and belief transform before their eyes. Civilizations rise and fall during a vampire's lifetime, and the sorrows and sense of loss and isolation that accompany this are things a human mind likely cannot comprehend. It is shocking enough for some of our human friends to go back to their home towns and see that mini-malls have sprouted where their little league baseball field used to stand.

Different cultures have different views on eternity. Even in this day and age, becoming a vampire is not considered socially acceptable on the whole. Most vampires, even those turned in the twentieth and twenty-first centuries, find themselves ostracized by their friends and family, and this is even truer for vampires that were turned thousands of years ago.

The only time in which vampirism was considered perfectly acceptable, even the norm, was in scattered tribes among the nomadic hunter-gatherers sometime around 8500 BC. It appears that humans and vampires coexisted in tribes and survived by forming symbiotic relationships: The vampires would feed on the blood of the felled prey, and the humans would consume the meat and foraged foodstuffs. In turn, the humans would also allow the vampires to feed off of them lightly, although not to the point of death, and in the end, both halves of the tribe would mutually sustain one another, especially in times of near famine. These mixed-vampiric tribes would simply not have to hunt or forage with as much urgency as the all-human tribes.

However, those times of vampiric tribal hunting are long past, and with the advent of agrarian and industrial civilization, the abandonment of the ways of the Paleolithic hunter-gatherers, and the spread of the vampiric pathogen to those who weren't as inclined to peaceful feeding as the nomads, vampires found themselves gradually driven underground. The dawn of agriculture left little place for those who feed on blood—especially human blood—and humans began to perceive vampires as pests and predators akin to, and little better than, feral wolves or rats.

The vampires' inverted circadian rhythms and their need to exist only at night gave birth to further fear and apprehension among human settlements. After the relationship between humans and vampires of the hunter-gather period dissolved, humans no longer saw a use for them, as they had during ancient times. Vampires were an unknown quantity, and humans fear the unknown. Humans evolved to live almost entirely during sunlight hours out of necessity. They needed to tend the fields and the livestock during the day, and woke at dawn to do so. Night was a time of danger and uncertainty; leaving the safety of a settlement's fires in the evening left humans vulnerable to predators and bandits, and human eyes were not built to see clearly in the darkness. Certainly the vampires' aversion to daylight and biological need to emerge only during nighttime gave more fuel to fearsome speculation regarding their nature, and further relegated them to the status of heartless hunters.

Their ability to fearlessly walk in darkness, their vitality and strength, gave vampires the allure of having limitless freedom that humans did not possess. Envy does breed hatred as much as fear does. Vampires no longer fit neatly into our "civilized" society, so we began to perceive them as a threat and little else.

Although in Western culture, the idea of the vampire's eternal life brings a sort of decadence and beautiful decay with it, theocracies began to spring up that had little place for creatures with superhuman strength, extended lifespans, and the wisdom that often accompanies the latter. Scare tactics were employed by way of fireside tales and myths that were incorporated into the organized religions. These myths led to the worldwide ostracizing of our vampiric brethren, and through the ages, fear of them was inspired through misrepresentations, such as the *bhūta*, a living corpse that feeds on unsuspecting humans and animates other corpses with its touch; the *pennangalan*, with its horrific detachable head; the lightning-wielding *impundulu*; the deceptively beautiful *manananggal*; and even the *chupacabra*.

The nutrition requirements of a vampire have always been a source of horror to most humans. We like to perceive ourselves as being at the top of the food chain, with nothing to fear as long as we possess tools and weapons and the opposable thumbs necessary to wield them. We have been indoctrinated with the idea that we are the lords of all we survey, and it is shocking to most to have to come to terms with the cold, hard fact that there are creatures on this planet that are, essentially, bred to feed on us.

The horror we feel at the thought of being food, the envy we feel with regards to the vampire's extended lifespan, and the true nature of the vampire having been clouded in fearsome myth for millennia gave birth to many strange assumptions about vampires that have fed our fears. Though we have largely disregarded venerable myths in the twenty-first century, another strange phenomenon has occurred: Vampires have been reduced to allegory. The vampiric condition has been used as a metaphor for misogyny and addiction, unbridled eroticism, and gluttony.

All of this already saddles the vampire with an inordinate amount of emotional baggage, but we also have biological ramifications of the vampiric condition to consider. The vampire's inability to withstand daylight can lead to a depressive mood disorder similar to Seasonal Affective Disorder in humans, though it is significantly more pronounced, manifesting itself in a range spanning from dysthymia to major depressive episodes. The changes that occurred during the evolution of *Homo sapiens* into *Homo striga* created the vampire's inability to process solar radiation, but did not adequately compensate for the negative effects of a complete lack of exposure to sunlight. The neurons that produce and regulate dopamine, serotonin, and norepinephrine are, to one degree or another, adversely affected as a result, effectively making it more difficult for a vampire to achieve positive emotional states. However, it seems that these specialized neurotransmitters are stimulated during blood transfer with humans, which explains the vampire's general preference for human blood over that of other animals.

The mind reels at the thought of the agonies that a vampire has caused and borne witness to. The brutality of man against man and man against nature seem distant when read in a book or seen in a film. Experiencing horror after horror firsthand must twist and turn the soul. Centuries of war and torture seen during such a long and brutal existence as a vampire's could warp the heart and mind into a mass of dripping violence and furious vengeance. This can poison the soul, and it is not the vampire's fault, this incessant cruelty. It is the fault of mankind, who never learn the lessons of history, and who continue to scrabble over pieces of dirt or pointless ideologies.

Between the biological and sociological trials that a vampire faces, it is not hard to understand why they would be tragic and tortured.

Biblical Vampires

The Old Testament only makes a small reference to vampires. It is located in Leviticus 17:10–12 and 17:14 alongside ritual cleanliness, sin offerings and sacrifices, and shiqquwts, or abominations, including dietary and sexual prohibitions.

However, it is suspected that tales of vampires exist elsewhere in the Bible. Vampire historians have speculated that the Cities of the Plain, Sodom, Gomorrah, Admah, Zoar, and Zeboim, were Canaanite settlements where vampires were accepted into the general population. They lived much like their Neolithic ancestors, with humans and vampires coexisting in relative harmony. Over time, neighboring towns came to blame any disappearance, murder, or other act of violence or depravity on the people of the Cities, shadowing the five towns with an increasingly sinister reputation.

Now here you come, pretty little girl with your breasts pushed up in his face and smelling like a prime rib dinner. Oh sure, "He'll love me for me," you say! And you, Casanova, with your bravado and your too-cool swagger? "She'll want me more than she's wanted any other man!" Does your position not appear preposterous when you look at it from this angle, when you realize where your vampire has been and what he has seen? Are you not frightened just a little knowing

One fateful morning, three men were found exsanguinated on the banks of the River Jordan. Whether this was truly the act of a vampire, we may never know. The aftershock of the discovery, however, led to the desire for a scapegoat. A massive flash mob formed and terrorized the twin cities of Sodom and Gomorrah. A horrific day of arson, looting, plundering, and rioting took place, and both cities were completely destroyed, their populations decimated. The vampires of Admah, Zoar, and Zeboim fled for their lives and scattered throughout the Middle East. The tale of Sodom and Gomorrah was written as a symbol of the evils of vampirism and all the depravity that was attributed to their lifestyle. When she was turned into a pillar of salt, Lot's wife was being metaphorically punished for sympathizing with the vampires and turning back in compassion.

that a slight change in temperament can startle him into ripping your throat out with just two fingers to feast upon your life's vitality?

But you have met your vamp, you are smitten, and now you insist on dating him and enthralling him with your wiles. Will you watch as he feeds upon another? Will you help him procure victims for his need? What stance will you take?

Common Fallacies Concerning Vampires

It is the unknown we fear when we look upon death and darkness, nothing more. —Albus Dumbledore, *Harry Potter and the Half-Blood Prince*

Remember that we are talking about real-life vampires, not the mythological creatures molded by the tropes of literature, folktales, or film, most of which are based on ancient, usually misconstrued lore. We are talking about, possibly, the man or woman of your dreams or nightmares. This is the twenty-first century, and we now know that vampires are as real as the sun, so let's buckle down and deal with some actual information. It's time to play a little true or false.

TRUE OR FALSE? *Vampires are inherently mentally ill.* False, but the strain of the physical transformation brought on by the vampiric pathogen, the physical and mental demands of the vampiric state, and the pain of centuries of entropy and loss could easily unhinge some weaker-minded vampires. The Transeo and Interfectors (types of vampires described later in this volume) are certainly prototypical psychopaths. Even the most well-adjusted vampire is likely dealing with difficulties in adjusting to human society, anxiety over his or her condition, and a great deal of internal conflict. It is a challenging state of being (but then, so is being human).

In the early twentieth century, three vampire students of Carl Jung's opened a clinic in Zurich, the Internationale Gesellschaft für Vampirpsychotherapie, that specializes in applied analytical psychology for vampires in order to help them cope with the complexities of vampire unlife and adjust to rapidly changing times and attitudes. These vampire analysts provided a haven for troubled vampires seeking solace and counsel, as well as a center for educating vampire psychotherapists, psychologists, and psychiatrists.

Truth be told, many humans are nuts, so why can't a few vampires be mad too?

TRUE OR FALSE? *Vampires are spawns of Satan. They run amok spreading evil wherever they go.* False. Wow, is this thought crazy or what? Why would you think vampires were evil just because most of them feed on humans to sustain their own lives? Vampires, by and large, are no more evil than lions, jaguars, pythons, humans, or any other predators. They, like all of us, do what they must to survive.

TRUE OR FALSE? *Vampires are reanimated corpses and are immortal.* False. Oh please, are you starting to confuse them with zombies? One sure way to determine the difference is the sniff test. Zombies are rotted corpses and smell like…well, rotted corpses. Vampires, on the other hand, are reanimated dead folks who can't shower or be in running water, so they smell like…well, rotted corpses. There, see the difference? (We jest!)

TRUE OR FALSE? *Drinking blood is an addition to the vampire's diet and not a necessity.* False. Really wrong this time. Blood is not an energy drink for these folks. No sir, they really need it to stay alive.

TRUE OR FALSE? *Vampires are descended from Cain's bloodline (or Lilith's, or Judas').* False. Much like there is no proof of intelligent design, there is no verifiable evidence to corroborate the rumor that the origins of vampires lie in a Biblical curse. To the best of modern scientific knowledge, the pathogen that led to creation of the species *Homo striga* originated somewhere around 9800 BC during the Neolithic Revolution. While some humans were beginning to domesticate plants and livestock, those who lived in barren, untenable regions faced extinction. In order to survive, their bodies slowly mutated existing pathogens into ones that would cause permanent biological changes that helped facilitate their survival in unfruitful climes.

TRUE OR FALSE? *A human will necessarily become a vampire if bitten by one.* False. The transference of the actual vampiric pathogen, the one that truly turns a human into a vampire, is a dangerous process, and the pathogen is rarely transmitted by accident. Once in a very great while, a human will contract the virus on first contact with vampiric blood, saliva, or semen. However, in most cases, a vampire must drain and replace more than 70 percent of a human's blood repeatedly over the course of 12 to 24 hours. The blood is drained from the human, and then the vampire makes an incision in one of their own major arteries. The human must orally ingest the vampire blood from that wound. The comingled blood enters the system through the stomach, triggering both the initial resistance and the primary DNA modifications. If successful, the vampire pathogen will be transmitted, the human's DNA will begin to evolve, and he or she will begin transforming into a vampire within 24 to 48 hours. The complete process of transformation takes roughly five to seven days, depending on the strength of the human host's resistance.

It takes three to five non-fatal blood-to-blood or saliva-to-blood transferences in order to create a thrall (a vampire's devoted attendant). The number of transferences needed to create a thrall is determined by the human's susceptibility to the addictive properties present in vampire blood and saliva.

TRUE OR FALSE? *Vampires can only be killed by a wooden stake to the heart.* False. While vampires are stronger and more resilient than humans, they are vulnerable to a number of attacks, including exposure to sunlight, beheading, and evisceration, if the heart is removed from the chest cavity.

TRUE OR FALSE? *Vampires subsist entirely on human blood.* False. The harsh truth is that vampires are obligatory hematophagous (blood-feeding) creatures, wholly sanguivorous (subsisting upon blood), and it is impossible for them to digest any other type of food. However, vampires simply need the blood lipids and proteins of other mammalian creatures—not necessarily humans—in order to find sustenance, and they must consume approximately 7 percent of their body weight in blood roughly every 72 hours.

In reality, it is more sensible for a vampire to consume a small amount of blood, leaving the victim alive and able to replenish their natural blood supply so the vampire can feed on the same victim multiple times. Fortunately for the victim, the anticoagulant found in vampire saliva, which is related to draculin, is a serotonin-norepinephrine-dopamine-releasing agent that stimulates the release of oxytocin in the victim and causes an almost delirious euphoria. This euphoria is pleasantly incapacitating and enables the vampire to feed without struggling.

Vampire saliva also stimulates blood flow in the victim, which often mimics sexual arousal. In other words, there are definitely positive side effects of letting your mate feed on you occasionally.

It is not necessary for the blood vampires consume to be human, nor is it necessary for a vampire to completely exsanguinate their victims or to slay them outright. If the latter were true, using the simple mathematical principle of geometric progression, it is logical to deduce that all mammals would have died out within a few centuries of the onset of the vampire pathogen. Consequentially, the vampires, too, would have become extinct for lack of a food source. Many vampires opt for cattle blood, or the blood of other herd animals, in lieu of feeding on humans. The blood is healthiest for a vampire if it comes fresh, straight from the host.

In addition to basic nutrition, there are other primary health concerns that create vampires' need for blood. The vampire pathogen creates a condition similar to beta-thalassemia, a blood disorder, which in the case of vampires is relieved by the consumption of blood. Because of their peculiar hematological condition, their blood does not function wholly. Vampires must consume blood in order to regulate their body temperature, supply oxygen to their tissues, and purge their cardiovascular systems of urea, lactic acid, and other impurities.

TRUE OR FALSE? *Vampires cannot stand the smell of garlic.* Surprisingly this is true. Vampires never consume garlic, not just because of their aversion to the scent, but also because garlic's vasodilative effect, which causes dilation of the blood vessels, is injurious to them. In addition, allyl methyl sulfide, which cannot be digested, passes straight into the blood. This sulfide is harmless to humans, though it causes bad breath and unpleasant body odors; however, it causes debilitating gastrointestinal cramps and dermatitis in vampires.

A strange side effect of the vampire pathogen is an aversion to the scent of crushed garlic, which seems to be unrelated to the physical distress that the consumption of garlic causes. When crushed, garlic enzymes stored in the cell vacuoles of the bulb initiate the breakdown of several sulfur-containing compounds stored in vampires' cell fluids. The resulting pungent organosulfur compounds cause discomfort for vampires, with diallyl disulfide being the primary culprit.

TRUE OR FALSE? *Vampires must be invited into a home before they can cross the threshold.* False. This is a romantic idea, a reversal of the spider-and-fly interaction, but in reality, it is generally considered impolite to enter someone's home without being invited, vampire or not!

TRUE OR FALSE? *Vampires need to sleep with a lump of soil from their homeland or from the grave in which they were initially buried.* False. This an invention of Bram Stoker's, likely based on a vampire of small renown, Zigana Farkas. Born in the seventeenth century, Farkas was a pioneering olericulturist during a time when it was unheard of for women to work, much less possess an education or interest in science. She was shunned by her fellow villagers, and was accused of witchcraft because of her interest in agriculture. Vampirism came as her liberator. Her new lifestyle enabled her to continue her work in peace, and she began traveling all over the globe studying pedogenesis (soil formation) and the effects of unusual soils on plants, though she had lost the ability to consume the crops she studied.

Old habits die hard, and even vampires need hobbies: When Farkas moved back to Europe, she brought a significant amount of *terra preta* back with her from an excursion to the Guiana Highlands. She was something of a joke amongst her kin: Her story was related often, with snide amusement and derision, among Europe's haughty, aristocratic vampiric cabals. They held Zigana Farkas to embody everything they despised about rural vampires. Their sensibilities were strongly influenced by pre–French Revolution decadence and debauchery, and they felt that the time she spent on what they considered prosaic, boring, human interests was foolish and quite hickish.

This much-circulated tale was misinterpreted by Stoker, and another vampire legend was born. Many vampires since have used this myth in various forms to further the dramatic punch of their stories.

TRUE OR FALSE? *Vampires cannot abide the sight of the Christian cross.* This is an especially powerful moment in film versions of vampire stories, but it is false in real life. The vampire's condition is not spiritual in origin, and the evolution of *Homo striga* predates Abrahamic religion by a millennium. As a strange and ironic response to the perpetuation of this absurd legend, many vampires have adopted the use of religious iconography in their choices of personal and home decor.

TRUE OR FALSE? *Vampires cast no reflection.* False. This is partially based upon the use of silver to destroy another alleged shapeshifter—the werewolf. It has its roots in simple bigotry. Hearthside folkloric belief held that reflections seen in a mirror or other reflective surface were projections of the soul. Rumors perpetuated by the fear that many held for vampires merged with this belief over time and gave birth to this legend.

Vampires tend to be vain creatures, and it would be a travesty if they could not look at themselves in a mirror from time to time.

TRUE OR FALSE? *Vampires do not age.* True. Once an individual contracts the vampire pathogen, they cease to age. Cellular senescence ceases altogether, and there is no longer any shortening of telomeres after a cell-division cycle. For all intents and purposes, a vampire is immune to natural aging, and will not die unless slain by external means.

TRUE OR FALSE? *Becoming a vampire is irreversible.* True. Unfortunately, there is no "cure" for the vampiric pathogen. It is akin to a sudden and irreversible leap in an evolutionary chain.

Do All Children of the Night Think Alike?

The fact is that a vampire is not ruled by thinking. When a vampire believes that he thinks, he usually merely feels; and his instincts and feelings are powerful precisely in the proportion that they are irrational and undeniable. Reason reveals the other side, and knowledge of that other side can be absolutely fatal to the driving power of an instinct.
—Del Howison, *Dark Delicacies*

Consider all of your friends, those from school or work or just around the neighborhood whom you see on a daily basis while conducting your personal business. Now throw in all of your family members and relatives. Let's say we could toss them all into a big jar and put the lid on it and shake it up. Shake it up well. Now unscrew the top and pour everyone out. Separate them into groups by the way they think.

Wait! What? You say that there would only be one person in each group? Well, you are correct. Everyone thinks differently.

The way we think is a product of many things: how and where we were brought up, our experiences in life, the genes we inherited from our parents, etc. Those factors make us all think differently. We can agree on some things but never on everything. Vampires, like humans, are as unique as snowflakes. While there are some common threads among them, their customs, mannerisms, codes of etiquette, and preferences are influenced by their culture and upbringing. Also, like humans, they are influenced by the time or age in which they "lived"; this is simply more pronounced in vampires than in humans due to their prolonged lifespans.

Vampires were once humans. They had families and loved ones, jobs and responsibilities, places in their communities. They were not created out of thin air. But from there, everything else is different. They have had ages of experiences to shape their viewpoints and hone their skills. They have probably had more relationships than you have friends. Nobody ever accuses a vampire of being a virgin. Plus (and this is a big plus) *they have hunted and killed many, many humans.* They are predators, and even the gentlest of vampires still subsists on the blood of living creatures. You can see how their viewpoint might be a bit skewed from one another, and especially from your own.

Vampires are very strongly affected by the time period in which they were turned. With some exceptions, they have a tendency to cling to the attitudes of the era they were born into, and despite the many millennia that may have passed since they contracted vampirism, well, as they say, old habits die hard: A close friend of ours who was turned in 25 BC still clings to much of Ptahhotep's moral code, popular among ancient Egyptians, and many of our vampire associates from the Renaissance behave like a page out of Castiglione's etiquette guide, *Il Cortegiano*.

It is possible though, after spending enough time with a particular vampire that you may come to figure out how he thinks, or at least how he may act in a given situation. It would be to your advantage to accomplish this task. You know the old saying—*forewarned is forearmed*. But do vampires think in similar ways or patterns?

Some vampiric behavior may be due to the physical transformations that happen to the human brain upon death. The Uniform Determination of Death Act (UDDA), which has been adopted by most American states, defines "brain death" as the "irreversible cessation of all functions of the entire brain, including the brain stem." The experience of this profound and irreversible biological transformation must have had a profound effect upon the thinking processes of your intended romantic target.

While vampires are certainly very cerebral creatures, they are strongly driven by instinct and impulse, just as predatory animals in the natural world are. Vampires are propelled by animalistic impulses that are generated throughout their bodies as they spend each day of eternity in search of sustenance, food, and pleasure. Their needs are animal needs, but their desires are human desires.

This duality leads to one trait that is prevalent in all vampires, regardless of when they were turned. In essence, they all have had to develop a coping mechanism so that they are able to reconcile their humanlike consciences with their animal needs that must be met in order for survival. This ability is more pronounced in some vampires, while others seem to have little regard for their morality, but the same can be said to some degree about humans. There is good and bad in both types of creature. Throughout time there have been many humans whose taste for cruelty and wanton viciousness clearly outshone even the most depraved of vampires.

Nosferatu, Lord Ruthven, or Carmilla: What Sort of Vamp Are You Looking For?

A man's character is his fate.
—Heraclitus, *On the Universe*

As we've mentioned, there are as many different types of vampire personalities as there are human ones. After all, except for those few vampires who were born into their fate, all vampires were humans prior to becoming creatures of the night. In fact, were you to have met the vampire you are drawn to when he was in his human form, you may have been just as attracted to him then as you are now.

There have been quite a few scholars and historians among the vampire population, and over the centuries, repositories of their collective knowledge have been established all over the globe, the most notable libraries being in Vienna, Baghdad, Madrid, Kiev, Venice, Kyoto, Santo Domingo, Damascus, Thebes, and Detroit, though their specific locations remain shrouded in secrecy. Even in the twenty-first century, there is still very little trust between *Homo sapiens* and *Homo striga*, and vampires generally feel safer keeping their information among their own kind, so it is almost impossible for non-vampires to access the historical records. From time to time, however, information does leak out, and the following is partially based on Valentina Luzio's doctoral dissertation (Universita di Bologna, 1935) on intercultural vampire stereotypes, but it has also been pieced together through information we have gleaned through conversations with our vampire associates.

Over the centuries, vampires have classified their own kind, and in the past, these classifications became the root of a rough caste system that some vampires still adhere to today. For the most part, though, the terms are now used as loose slang, similar to the way that humans have coined phrases to describe those who share related predilections, tastes, and behaviors, such as *geek*, *goth*, *hippy*, or *tree-hugger*, although the vampiric terms encompass much more than tastes in music and clothing or sociological worldview. The terms of vampire classification that we have come across are *Cicuta, Interfector, Tombeur, Silenti, Transeo, Philologi, Misericordia* (also called *Tristus*), *Vespillo*, and *Sanctus*.

The Cicuta, also called the *Rictus*, are least likely to be accepted by human society, and are, sadly, also the least likely to be accepted by other vampires in general. Some vampires have a peculiar adverse reaction to the transference of the vampiric pathogen whereby their physical appearance is drastically altered: They lose their hair, their features become elongated, their eyes protrude, and a permanent and irreversible inflammation of their joints causes stiff movement and a clawlike rigidity in the hands and feet. Cicuta minds function as any other vampire's, but their appearance is so startlingly different that they find it almost impossible to find any acceptance whatsoever among humans or vampires. Usually these afflicted vampires choose to live in isolation, either on secluded estates or literally underground. Occasionally, small groups of Cicutas can be found cohabitating, finding comfort and companionship with those that share their condition. The Cicuta were parodied somewhat in F. W. Murnau's 1922 film *Nosferatu*.

There are two types of vampires that humans, and often other vampires, need to be wary of: the Interfectors and the Tombeur. The Interfectors are ruthless killers, ultimate hunters who view humans as livestock. They are brutal, but not necessarily cruel, and rarely toy with their prey. Universally, Interfectors perceive their transition into the vampiric state to be an initiation into a higher state of being, not transcendent or spiritual in nature, but rather a promotion to the top of the food chain.

Interfectors' cousins in savagery, the Tombeur, are much more complex in their hunting habits and their perceptions. In "The Vampire Maid," Hume Nisbet aptly describes a Tombeur's charged relationship with a human:

> *It was a rapid, distracting, and devouring infatuation that possessed me; all day long I followed her about like a dog, every night I dreamed of that white glowing face, those steadfast black eyes, those moist scarlet lips, and each morning I rose more languid than I had been the day before. Sometimes I dreamt that she was kissing me with those red lips, while I shivered at the contact of her silky black tresses as they covered my throat; sometimes that we were floating in the air, her arms about me and her long hair enveloping us both like an inky cloud, while I lay supine and helpless.*

Like the Interfectors, Tombeurs perceive their vampirism to be an initiation into a higher state of being and relegate humans to base foodstuffs. Unlike the Interfectors, however, the Tombeur are not straightforward predators, and there is a secondary purpose to their hunt: sexual gratification. They take full advantage of their saliva's hypnotic and psychotropic effects on humans, the mystique that surrounds vampires, the seemingly unnatural attraction some humans have toward vampires, and the potency of the Tombeurs' own sexual drive to lure humans into complex carnal relationships that culminate in feeding. They are consummate seducers, and some Tombeur feed, completely and terminally, on their conquests, while others create henchmen that are little more than sex slaves. Neither fate is something we would recommend to any of our readers.

The Silenti reject human society completely, and are, quite literally, the living dead. Either due to trauma, sociopathic psychological conditions they possessed while human, or through a desire to embrace this peculiar aesthetic, they adopt many of the stereotypes and trappings of the vampire-as-undead. Some act as monstrous killers, akin to the murderous ways of Interfectors, while others are more peaceable, but no less strange. E. F. Benson vividly describes a Silenti, in "The Room in the Tower" as:

> *Mrs. Stone as I had seen her last in my dreams: old and withered and white-haired. But in spite of the evident feebleness of body, a dreadful exuberance and vitality shone through the envelope of flesh, an exuberance wholly malign, a vitality that foamed and frothed with unimaginable evil. Evil beamed from the narrow,*

leering eyes; it laughed in the demon-like mouth.
The whole face was instinct with some secret and
appalling mirth; the hands, clasped together on
the knee, seemed shaking with suppressed and
nameless glee.

Most of these demonic vampires choose to live in crypts, haunting graveyards like proverbial ghouls. Many vampire death cults have sprung from the philosophies and writings of Silenti, including the House of Azrael, whose members venerate death itself as the supreme deity and oblivion as heaven.

Not all vampires are inherently dangerous, and in our experience, we have found that in this day and age, the Interfectors, Silenti, and Tombeur are blessedly rare. Most vampires that are encountered nowadays are Transeo, Misericordia, and occasionally Vespillo.

The Transeo are vampires that have assimilated into human society, often reaching positions of power. Among the Transeo there are many celebrated politicians, scientists, businessmen, philosophers, artists, writers, and musicians, and, surprisingly, a large number of influential clergy and militarists. Not every Transeo is an illustrious public figure; many simply desire the comforts associated with reentering society. In the past, most Transeo posed as humans as best they could, concealing their true natures. In the twenty-first century, more and more Transeo are coming out in the open, and they form the backbone of most vampire-acceptance movements.

The Misericordia, or Tristis, are vampires that are consumed with a longing to regain their lost humanity, some to the point of being driven mad by the desire to be human once more. The shock of their transition into vampirism and the rejection they faced from friends and loved ones was devastating, and it compromises their ability to find solace and comfort. Unlike the Transeo, Misericordia cannot merge into human society, but are relegated by their own grief to the position of outsiders. Their inherent melancholy and morose temperaments make it difficult for them to cultivate relationships with either humans or vampires. Most vampires treat the Misericordia with a fair amount of derision, and they are sometimes hunted by Interfectors who see the perspective of the Misericordia as an affront to their way of thinking.

The Philologi are scholars and philosophers that have dedicated themselves to the pursuit of knowledge, utilizing their extended lifespan to further their research. They are usually reclusive, and some were once Transeo that have rejected the bustle of human society in favor of solitude.

The Vespillo are dedicated to assisting newly infected vampires in understanding and accepting their condition and learning to live with the challenges that vampires face. Vespillo, like the Transeo, tend to become members of vampire-acceptance movements, pushing for a wider understanding of vampires among the human population.

Other Types of Vampires as Represented in Myth & Legend

Asasabonsam: With metal teeth and hooked feet, these vampires are well suited to being James Bond movie villains. Hanging from trees in the African forests, they grab their victims with their feet and bring them up to "bite them on the thumb"!

Baital: Somewhat like the folklore of Carmilla, who transformed into a cat, or Dracula, able to become a dog, these Indian vampires are short and half-man/half-bat.

Bajang: These were beings in the form of weasels who were enslaved by Malaysian sorcerers and forced to kill many members of single families.

Baobhan: These vampires are similar to succubus in that they take the form of Scottish women who force men to dance with them unto exhaustion and then feed from them.

Ch'ing Shih: Similar to a will-o'-the-wisp, these Chinese demons' nonmaterial forms are that of glowing orbs of light. They kill with their deadly breath (much like an old math teacher I once had) and also suck the blood from their victims.

Civateteo: These Mexican witches attack young children and mate with their fathers to produce vampire children.

Dearg-Due: These Irish vampires can be killed by building a pile of stones over their grave. They cannot shape shift to escape.

Empusa: An ancient offshoot of the Incubus and Succubus (see below), these Grecian female demons are either young women or old hags.

Ekimmu: Erroneously referred to by Montague Summers as Assyrian vampires, these are ghosts looking for peace.

Incubus or Succubus: These are two different forms of European sexual vampires.

Jararaca: These are Brazilian snake vampires who drink the blood of sleeping women.

Kallikantzaros: Actually closer to werewolves than to humans, these vampires are born between Christmas and New Year's Day. When they are older, the Greeks believe, they will assume a half-man/half-animal shape between those same calendar periods and stalk their victims only to retreat down to Hell until the next year-end holiday.

Some other vampires in myth and legend from around the world include: **Avarcolac, Brucolacas, Dracul, Kalika, Kattakhanes, Khadro, Krvopijac, Kwakiytl, Lamia, Lobishomen, Loogaro, Mulo, Nachzerer, Ogolgen, Otgiruru, Owenga, Rakshasa, Sharabisu, Shtriga, Strigoi, Strigoi Vii, Strigoi Morti, Stryx, Vampir, Veshtitza, Vrykolakas,** and **Wampir.**

The Sanctus are considered by some pious vampires to be the saints of their kind, and from what we have gleaned, they are very likely the stuff of myth. These vampires are paragons that possess impossible, phenomenal powers that defy known physics, including the ability to shift shape, turn into a gaseous form, and command other vampires through will alone. The mythological Sanctus are venerated by some, but we have no evidence whatsoever that they truly exist.

The point is this: You should not under any circumstances believe that you understand your vampire after knowing them for only a short period of time. The personality and monstrous types that he or she could possibly be are way beyond your understanding. Take your time and tread very, very carefully.

Makers & Minions: Other Relationships You Need to Understand

Some people have so much respect for their superiors that have none left for themselves. —Peter McArthur

What do you gain by dating a vampire and what does the vampire gain by having a relationship with you? Why is it that most master-mistress or master-slave relationships end after relatively short periods of time? Are there longer-term commitments that need to be made and acted upon that usually get ignored? Or are we merely driven into these relationships for sexual reasons, and once those are taken care of the longer-term emotional commitments fall by the wayside?

You need to think these points through at the outset of your relationship with your vampire, as it is important that you know what he needs to get out of your dating commitment and that you make sure he understands what you need. Without these points being settled upon relatively early you may find your status changing from squeeze to supper! In order to determine what you both want out of your relationship, it is important to understand the ways in which vampires interact with their "kin."

In most "familial" vampiric relationships, one vampire is dominant and one is submissive. There is a symbiosis to most all such master-slave relationships. Each side needs the other. The submissive is dependent on his or her master for many things, particularly from a psychological point of view and sometimes for their very survival. It seems one-sided at first glance, but in truth, a dominant needs his or her submissive just as much. Healthy power exchange is always a balance. In all great bondage and discipline relationships, both participants enhance their emotional and psychological well-being through compliance and control.

The master-slave relationship is a common theme in literature and film because it is inside most of us to realize that in a consensual relationship, the right person can complete us, not because we cannot take care of ourselves, but because there is strength in numbers (especially when somebody has got your back). Plus, the relationship adds dimension and variation that creates a larger emotional spectrum for us as individuals. Would most of us survive without this copilot? Yes, of course. But many of us are happier just for the chance to share what we feel inside and who we are with another being.

Vampire society is a complex web. In some ways, it does have similarities to a human lineage or family tree, but it has ties that bind in ways that humans may find difficult to understand. The connection that we humans have with our parents, our siblings, and our distant relations is strong and many feel that blood ties within families transcend mere biology and are spiritual bonds. With vampires, though, the blood ties are literal and are not in any way a point of philosophical contention. The ephemeral, metaphorical links between humans cannot match the connection that vampires have with their Makers and their progeny.

Each vampire could, theoretically, trace his or her lineage back throughout the ages to the first vampires that emerged during Neolithic times. As of this writing, several well-respected geneticists from the Ravan Institute in Varanasi, India, led by the venerable vampire Dr. Usha Avinash, are utilizing genome-mapping technology to literally trace the vampire bloodlines to their origins and map their migration and infection patterns throughout history. A vampiric bloodline and the semimythological progenitor of a bloodline are both referred to by the same term, *kelda*, which translates from Old Norse to mean "spring, or well."

At the crown of a vampire's immediate family tree sits his or her Maker. This refers, somewhat obviously, to the individual who transmitted the virus. The Maker's offspring are referred to as children, progeny, parvulus, or, archaically, garor, as, in times long past, a vampire's children were considered to be his "Garden of Souls."

In defiance of all current scientific understandings of viral epidemiology and pathogenic microbial agents, the vampiric pathogen, when transmitted, creates an intense emotional and psychological bond between the two parties. This bond provides both the Maker and the progeny retrocognition of the other's life, as though they were their own memories, and a sort of limited bilocation, in which the vampires can experience sensory and emotional responses firsthand, as though they had limited access to the mind of the other vampire. Both of these abilities manifest in different, seemingly arbitrary, intensities, though the connection is most acute during times of extreme stress. This psychological intimacy is almost impossible for a human to understand. It provides the Maker with an enormous amount of access to their progeny's memories, feelings, and desires, leaving their offspring, particularly those in the early stages of vampirism, extremely vulnerable to manipulation. Some Makers use this to their advantage, leaving bitter, lonely, resentful children in their wake. However, many Makers cultivate a more positive filial relationship with their progeny.

In any case, in the connection a vampire feels with his or her Maker, powerful emotions are inevitably involved, be they feelings of love or hate. Circumstances and personalities dictate how the relationship evolves. Regardless of how your vampire feels about his or her Maker, or his or her own progeny, it is of utmost importance that you respect the bond that they share. Even a vampire who hates his Maker with an unrivaled passion would demand that you show respect to the one that made them what they are today.

The length of time that progeny spends with their Maker varies depending on the nature of their relationship, the nature of personalities involved, and the Maker's motivation in creating his or her children. On one end of the spectrum, most Interfectors and other comparatively malevolent and sociopathic vampires will create children and immediately abandon them, even before the vampiric pathogen has completely taken hold. Tombeur (and some Interfectors) often create children to act as extensions of their will, and their progeny are little more than bonded slaves. Gentler, more humane vampires tend to create progeny out of love or a desire for companionship. These relationships are usually warm, at least for a time, and these children usually spend many hundreds of formative years with their makers before they strike out on their own. The level of care and instruction that a fledgling vampire receives is also subject to these variables.

Vampire Blood, Thralls, and Addiction

A current theory in the scientific community argues that humans who have been given enough vampire blood to qualify them for minion status have a physical addiction to the blood and saliva of vampires, which contributes to their willingness to act in a servile position to the vampire in order to fulfill the needs of their addiction. The pharmacologic phenomenon of tolerance is not present, and the soporific and euphoric effects of vampire's blood on the same test subject do not seem to diminish over time.

Factors such as an individual's genetic and psychological susceptibility to the pleasure-releasing agents in vampire blood and saliva are determining factors in whether or not a human is predisposed to addiction.

To a much lesser extent, vampires share a similar, though considerably weaker, bond with their brothers and sisters—those who were also turned by the same Maker. As with human siblings, there are rivalries among some and affection between others. Again, it depends on the circumstances and personalities involved.

Master-slave relationships also exist between vampires and their thralls. A thrall, also called a minion, ghoul, henchman, or preta, is a human who has become addicted to vampire blood. As we mentioned previously, a thrall is bound psychochemically to a vampire. Thralls, generally, were deemed unfit for turning, and also unfit for a companionship among equals. Usually, thralls are humans who are lackeys or hangers-on—something akin to a groupie—and they command little respect from the vampires they latch on to. The bond is decidedly one-sided; most vampires view their thralls as domestics, and the tralls are often beneath a vampire's notice. Scientists have found that the *substantia nigra* (a brain structure located in the midbrain that helps regulate mood and is also instrumental in the motivation, reward, and addiction cycles of the brain) is over stimulated in thralls, and it is hypothesized that their increased vulnerability to addiction coupled with the euphoria-inducing, narcotic effects of vampire blood further seals their bond with their vampire.

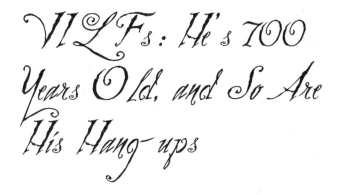

VILFs: He's 700 Years Old, and So Are His Hang-ups

The tragedy of old age is not that one is old, but that one is young. —Oscar Wilde, *The Picture of Dorian Gray*

A relationship between vampires and humans truly is the most extreme of May-December romances. He has lived through the entire history of mankind (maybe). The vampire has an enormous range of experiences to draw upon, and they are shaped by millennia of upheaval, change, and adversity that is difficult for a human to comprehend.

A very interesting thing will occur when you meet your vampire, the one who makes your heart go pitter-pat. The odds are that your new mate will be at least a century older than you are, and in the truest sense of the word, chivalry will be undead. Younger vampires are extremely vulnerable, and it takes many, many years for a man or woman to adjust to life-in-undeath. It is unlikely that any vampire under the age of 100 is someone who you will be able to make a connection with. In all likelihood, the vampire will have a much broader scope of knowledge than you have been able to accumulate during your relatively brief life. If he does not, you'd better let him go. At best, such a vampire is unable or unwilling to utilize his extended lifespan for self-improvement and the quest for knowledge. At worst, he is a fool with no passion for life. If he doesn't possess more experience and understanding than you do, he is either hopelessly obtuse or he's playing some sort of game, feigning ignorance to help reel you into his clutches.

For humans, overcoming behaviors that have been cultivated over decades is difficult. Our upbringing, the culture and country in which we lived, the influence of society and of our friends and families: All these things contribute to our behavior patterns, societal expectations and values, manners and mannerisms, and moral codes, and most certainly our views on relationships and gender. This is even truer for vampires.

Cultural differences may manifest themselves in little quirks held over from lifetimes in other eras. Darius, a Persian vampire acquaintance of ours who spent centuries living in Egypt after being turned, still, to this day, anoints all of his guests with oil when they visit his home; Alessio, a Tuscan vampire and close friend who was turned in the fifteenth century, lives his life like a page out of *Il Galateo*. Many of the Victorian vamps of our acquaintance still behave as quintessential gentlemen, down to the minutiae of good manners, such as passing on the right as they make their way down a sidewalk and sending written invitations at least a day in advance of any entertainment.

Presenting more of a challenge than quirks of custom and etiquette is the issue of gender equality. Which, for the most part throughout history, has rarely been the norm. You should consider ahead of time whether you can handle a mate whose ideal woman comes straight out of the *Good Wife's Guide* of the 1950s, or a vampire who may quote Athenian dramatist Menander at you as you pursue your second doctorate ("Teaching a woman to read and write? What a terrible thing to do! Like feeding a vile snake on more poison!"). Conversely, a Neolithic vampire, a vampire that was a Brittonic tribesman, or a vampire that hails from ancient Egypt or Mesopotamia will be likely to respect gender equality, and a Spartan or Sarmatian vampire, or a vampire that hails from a matriarchal African tribe, would expect their mates to be their absolute equals, both in love and war. As Herodotus said of the Sarmatians, the women are "frequently hunting on horseback with their husbands; in war taking the field; and wearing the very same dress as the men" and further emphasizing their belief in the strength and power of women, "No girl shall wed till she has killed a man in battle." Are you up for assisting your mate with the hunt?

However, if your vampire holds the aforementioned beliefs that women are second-class citizens, your only chances for domination or even equalization are your looks and personality. There won't be a trick he doesn't know, a deception he hasn't played, or a lie he has never heard. His experiences give him a unique street-wisdom, and it takes a shrewd, quick-witted, observant mind to survive the millennia.

As shallow as it may seem, the truth is that your looks are your main trump card. You do not have to be a model; you simply have to fascinate, captivate, and seduce. All men and women are capable of this. A vampire is a sensualist by nature, and most are near-obsessed with beauty in all its myriad forms. What you actually need are ways to lower the defensive personality guards that he has put up over decades of time living among humans. He can shield himself with the knowledge that he has picked up over numerous years of survival, and he can change his behavior.

But the things he cannot change are his desires and needs, romantic, sexual, and survival. His urges still pull mightily inside him, like the tides of the oceans. They pull even stronger than in a human male because the vampire is tied so inexorably to the phases of the moon. He needs to feel the warmth of your body and the blood pulsating through your veins as your heartbeat quickens in anticipation of a tryst with him. He needs to feel himself inside you while your body grasps him like a glove of human flesh. He needs this comfort, and you have to be sure that you are the only one who is providing it.

Where Is the Lair?

The home is not the one tame place in the world of adventure.
It is the one wild place in the world of rules and set tasks.
—G. K. Chesterton

While the coffin or crypt is considered *de rigueur*, a vampire's lair isn't always a funerary box, though many vampires do still utilize them as a style choice that's in keeping with the mythology that has sprouted around their kind, thanks to popular fiction. As with almost anyone you will meet during your dating life, they will already have a home, a house, or a lair, someplace where they can crash for the day, and where your vampire lays his head will give you valuable information about him.

A vampire's primary concern with regard to his lair is purely health-related: The electromagnetic-radiation spectrum that sunlight emits is physically harmful. While some closed-minded and puritanical individuals believe that the vampire's aversion to sunlight is a religious allegory of sorts that illustrates the wrath of God or some such nonsense, the truth is that the vampire's skin cannot process ultraviolet rays in the same fashion that human skin can, and prolonged exposure to the sun's radiation breaks down the DNA structure of the vampire's unique blood type. Exposure to sunlight does not cause the sudden and dramatic conflagration popularized in fiction (although that looks really cool in movies); the effects of sunlight on a vampire's blood is akin in some ways to the effects of nuclear radiation on humans. In addition, the vampire's skin's susceptibility to photo damage is acute. Over time, exposure to the sun causes permanent cell death, from the dermis inward, resulting in necrosis or death due to the cells' loss of reproductive ability.

As such, vampires choose to sleep in areas that are sealed completely from sunlight, and their choices of resting place are as varied as their personalities. In our travels, we have met vampires that utilize contemporary panic rooms, abandoned bomb shelters, and bank vaults, as well as mansions and townhouses. Most vampires have access to a considerable amount of money, and many have specially built, completely secure subterranean rooms within their homes. Scientifically inclined vampires may utilize a pyrheliometer to accurately measure the solar radiation flux density within their lair to ensure their safety, but most do away with such extreme obsessiveness.

So for vampires, their home is a matter of life and death. The last thing you will be able to do is jump in and "spruce it up" a little. Tread lightly, and do not push to see their abode. If so inclined, they will, over a period of time, invite you to their place of safety.

Where their "crypt" is located says a lot about how confident they may or may not be about their abilities as a vampire and to get around unnoticed in human civilization. Geographically, vampires can be found anywhere in the world. Although it is rare to find vampires living in countries north of the polar circle during the time of the midnight sun, during their months of darkness, Arctic settlements have been very popular with vampires. However, Nordic vampires must exercise extreme caution when venturing forth, even during the darker months. Though UV radiation is comparatively weak during dawn and twilight, fresh snow can reflect as much as 80 percent of the sun's rays, so even in dimmer light, vampires may be exposed to high amounts of solar radiation. Tromsø, Norway, for example, is a contradiction of sorts. From April until August, the city has traditionally been a haven for those seeking to flee a vampire's wrath, while from late November to January, it is a sanctuary for *Homo striga*.

In other words, for all practical purposes, a vampire's lair is the Bat Cave. Not only is it his place of rest, but it is also where he plots and schemes, advancing his convoluted machinations. In his lair, he is protected from prying eyes and is safeguarded against the perils of solar radiation and human interference. If you are lucky enough to visit a vampire domicile, take a good look around. Think about its location and consider the following questions things, as their answers will all point out some personality pluses or minuses in your dark one's desires:

Is the lair near an urban area? In one respect, this would allow the vampire easier pickings come feeding time and may even help them to keep their hungry eyes away from you. On the other hand, it may make the chance of discovery a more probable occurrence. Have they weighed both options well?

Is the lair above ground or subterranean? One might think it is traditional for the home or crypt to be below the ground. Some of this comes from our old thinking about cemeteries and such. But consider the fact that vampires can't live in or even cross running water. Seldom would they have that problem if they lived in a place that were aboveground.

What is the window situation? We all know the vampire's problem with sunlight. Will they have to remember to close curtains or shut the shades every morning? At night when they are entertaining you at home, will passersby or neighbors be able to see into the lit quarters?

Does your vampire own their own place, having been successful in the passing years or centuries of gathering money? This would allow them to customize their lair in any manner they saw fit. If they are renting or leasing, or even if they stay with you and you are renting or leasing, there is always the possibility of a nosey landlord ruining things for everyone concerned.

It is also important to remember that the numerous locks, alarms, and other safety precautions that vampires utilize in their sleeping spaces are not to keep you out and are not even simple matters of desiring privacy or solitude. They are matters of safety, period.

Pros & Cons of Dating the Undead

We boil at different degrees. —Clint Eastwood

So you think you're sold on dating a vampire, but what about other creatures of the night? Simply put, if you were interested in dating a human, you would not be reading this book. As far as mates go, disembodied spirits, zombies, werewolves, and humans all have their pluses and minuses.

Disembodied spirits can be entertaining, and we have rarely met a girl who has been disappointed by a nocturnal tryst with an incubus. However, it is extremely difficult to form long-lasting relationships with incorporeal beings. Ghosts are irrevocably stuck in the violence of the moment they were killed and will spend most of their time relating the details of the incident *ad nauseum.* Conversations with ghosts tend to be one-sided streams of consciousness. Ghosts have no care for the future and are notoriously scatterbrained. Any semblance of domestic bliss is usually out of the question, particularly with poltergeists, and if you value your grandmother's china, it's best to keep these guys out of the house.

Zombies are just plain messy, and they are only interested in one thing: brains. Realize, however, that it isn't any big loss, as they really have nothing to offer.

Humans? If you want to date a human, you are best served by signing up with an online dating service, though it is not uncommon to find zombies there, too.

However, the werewolf's curse is different. If you're not sure that a vampire is the right monster for you, a werewolf would likely be the next place you would turn. Werebeasts tend to be extremely clannish, gravitating to their own out of a desire for safety and a loyalty to their community. They are an emotionally volatile, primal, and extremely violent species, and are noted for their pagan piety. Because of their insular nature, werebeasts rarely choose a mates without infecting them with lycanthropy. While there is a great deal of wild freedom to be found in werebeast society, it is a condition best left to nature lovers and rural types. Urban werebeasts are uncommon and often find themselves uncomfortable in polite society. As opposed to being a part of daily life, the werewolf's curse recurs on a monthly cycle. (Hmmm…

The Aequitas Foundation

One of the first vampire attorneys to publicly declare her vampirism, Ekuwa Adutwumwaa Adofo, a Philologi, founded the Aequitas Foundation along with Sandalio Mahin Romero, a prominent werewolf tribal leader from the mountains of Aragon. The Aequitas Foundation works to educate the vampire and lycanthrope communities about the laws that are in place to protect their kinds as well as to protect human society from vampiric and lycanthrope depredations, helping to create a safe environment in which all can coexist.

Ms. Adofo is the preeminent vampire champion of human rights and has campaigned to ensure that the penal codes of each country are expanded to include vampire and lycanthrope crimes of violence; she is particularly vigilant with regards to the savage acts perpetrated by Interfectors and Transeo. Although she also fights against hate crimes directed at vampires, her activism for human and lycanthrope rights have made her exceedingly unpopular with some facets of the vampire community. As a result, she is almost always accompanied by her bodyguards, the twin lycanthropes Atá Pánin and Ataá Kúmaa, three of her most loyal progeny (also attorneys), and her pack of Schutzhund-trained side-striped jackals.

We wonder where this tale had its beginning?) The vampire, on the other hand lives with his curse every day (or should we say night?) of his existence.

Both the curse of the werewolf and that of the vampire allow for special attributes that help offset any awkwardness of the conditions. Vampires enjoy far superior strength, agility, speed, stamina, and senses compared to normal humans, as well as the ability to heal any injuries with incredible speed. They are impervious to almost all forms of disease, expect for leprosy. Werewolves also enjoy increased strength, speed, agility, and stamina. Vampires have a heightened sense of smell, as do werewolves, who also have a heightened sense of hearing. So far, it is fairly even except for that nagging time-lag thing.

If a werewolf catches the odor of fresh blood, or if it is the time of the blood moon, the first full moon after the harvest moon, his primal instincts become uncontrollable and he spirals into a feeding frenzy. For this hairy beast, the transformation will begin as soon as the full moon rises completely above the horizon. He doesn't even have to look at it—it needs only to happen. His body goes through a rapid, agonizing series of changes. While transformed, he has absolutely no control over his body, and his entire existence begins to revolve around the thrill of the hunt and the desire to feed. While these points may hold their own form of attraction for you as a prospective date or mate, for most folks, they are at least minor red flags.

Any creature that the werewolf bites or scratches but does not kill will carry the burden of the same curse.

If your attraction to a werewolf can overcome the physical repercussions of his curse, the biggest problem with your wolf boy is that as soon as daylight starts popping its head above the horizon, he will revert back to his human form and have no recollection of the events that took place during his transformation. It's very much like a drinking binge. So much for eternal love. If you find a way to overcome a werewolf's little memory problem, you just might have a good life together.

However, don't be so quick to dismiss the vampire's charms. He can enthrall humans with irresistible charisma. There is an incomparable connection when two people are bound in blood, especially if you eventually join your mate in undeath. Together, the two of you will then be entwined throughout all time. You share a real piece of each other, blood and soul.

Part Two

How to Date a Vampire:

The Etiquette & the Information

How to Dress for a Vampire

A sweet disorder in the dress
Kindles in clothes a wantonness
—Robert Herrick, *"Delight in Disorder"*

In motion pictures and books, vampires are often described as what can only be called "dandies," dressed in formal wear. In actuality, it does a vampire absolutely no good to stand out in a crowd in such a way. In fact, a vampire desires exactly the opposite. He wants the ability to blend in with humans. As with a drove of sheep, the last thing the vampire desires is to appear the wolf. Consequently, he will dress in everyday clothing best suited to the situation at hand. Those who lay claim to being vampires and dress outlandishly or in extreme Victorian or Edwardian apparel can almost assuredly be pointed out as phonies who want to take on the vampiric mystique without having the knowledge of how to actually do so. However, the same cannot be said of a vampire's companion, who should dress to attract not only his eyes but the eyes of the crowd as well so as to take attention away from him.

Vampires are sensualists, and physical beauty is, to most of their kind, paramount in their initial attraction to humans. This may seem shallow, but it is simply an indication of their unique psychochemistry, which leads to an almost childlike fascination with the sensual pleasure of aesthetic stimulation. A vampire's concept of beauty is often influenced strongly by the time period, geographical location, and culture in which they lived as humans, so when dressing to charm your vampire, you'll want to consider the type of body shape and facial features that were considered prized in their particular era and also use cosmetics, fashions, and accessories that were popular in his the vampire's lifetime.

You should dress with the same intentions you would in order to attract a warm-blooded human mate. Be alluring yet tasteful, and most importantly, be yourself. Do not try to be overtly sexual in your attire, either. If you dress well, your sexuality will burst through without excessively revealing garments. Instead of offering up your "goods," as it were, with a plunging neckline or too-tight trousers, be more conservative in your attire and exhibit some dignity and grace in your presentation. Style is key, as vampires have, generally, developed extremely refined tastes over the centuries. Pique his or her interest without selling yourself cheaply. Being alluring without being overtly sexual grants you some small measure of control, and you will need all the control you can muster if this relationship is to end with something other than you losing your arterial virginity.

When you first meet your vampire, you'll have no idea if he likes current fashion the best, or maybe something that speaks to his memories of ancient Egypt or precolonial Zimbabwe. Once you do get to know him a little, do some digging. Many vampires, whether or not they choose to admit it, harbor a secret fondness for their homelands, and for the eras in which they lived their human lives. This innate, ingrained nostalgia is something to be aware of in both your social interactions with vampires and in something as seemingly mundane as your choices of attire when you are on the hunt. Remember: We see with our eyes before we see with our hearts.

However, it is not necessary, or advisable, for you to fully outfit yourself in historically accurate accoutrements from eras past in order to catch a vampire's eye. This would certainly be over the top and considered gauche, unless it was within an appropriate environment, such as a costume ball. Subtlety is key in the art of love, be it with vampires or with other humans. Many modern fashions take their cues from other times, and it is easy to cleverly incorporate a little bit of history in your mode of dress or choice of hair and make-up.

Ungirdled tunics and draped shawls would likely appeal to a vampire of ancient Assyria, while a sleeveless, straight-waisted *garçonne*-style dress would catch the eye of a vampire turned in the 1920s. Platform shoes mimic chopines, and corsets, widely utilized throughout Europe and North America in the sixteenth through nineteenth centuries, are extremely popular in current fashion. Kohl-rimmed eyes may pique an Egyptian vampire's interest, and an elaborate updo might catch the eye of a vampire from Louis XIV's court.

Vampires are consummate sensualists, and their condition lends to a heightened sense of touch. Bearing this in mind, you can also utilize textiles whose textures are reminiscent of fabrics from a vampire's homeland and generation. Flowing, finely embroidered, elegantly draped silks may enchant a twelfth century Japanese Hōjō Regency vampire, while bold brocades would appeal to a Byzantine vampire.

When dressing to impress, also try to be aware of the social mores of a vampire's era. A belle époque vampire would be delighted by a bit of exposed décolletage and dramatic flair, and an Egyptian Fourth Dynasty vampire would be at ease with the scantiest of outfits. A Mesopotamian vampire will generally be as sexually open as an enlightened modern vamp, while a vampire that hails from medieval Europe or colonial America may be significantly more conservative. Take this into consideration when you are debating how much skin to expose and how tight your bodice should be.

In the midst of all this, keep one thing in mind: Don't overdo it. We repeat—*Don't overdo it.*

Although you'll want to dress to your vampire's tastes, outfitting yourself as a stereotypical media-inspired vampire is often considered vulgar, as are the trappings of too-pale makeup and anything else that smacks of vampire costuming clichés. Fake fangs and stage blood? Toss them out, unless you are deliberately trying to offend potential mates or doing a badly exaggerated vampire comedy sketch. Such things mark you as prey, not as partner.

Religious icons, specifically the crucifix, are considered to be in poor taste by most vampires, while some vampires embrace the irony of the stigma. Our advice is to skip such things altogether until you are far enough into the relationship to know better about your partner one way or the other. Onyx, garnets, and black diamonds are considered by some superstitious vampires to be boons of good fortune. It would not hurt to utilize these stones in your choices of jewelry.

Also think well of the placement of jewelry and accessories, as it can make all the difference when considering the practical aspects of dressing to impress a vampire. If you consent to your vampire feeding on you, is it something that you would both want to flaunt, or is it something you would rather keep between yourselves? If it is the former, a well-placed jewel will draw attention to that spot you want to show off; if the latter, chokers and scarves are a tasteful choice. That is, if your neck is where he feeds from.

However, this advice regarding physical beauty is in no way an attempt by us to urge you to be hypercritical of your physical features, nor is it a suggestion that you change yourself dramatically. There are myriad types of beauty, and a vampire's taste, while usually heavily influenced by their cultural upbringing, is as unique as a snowflake. But just be warned: A dirty, unkempt, sloppy mess of a person will only really appeal to a Cicuta (a vampire who was physically deformed when he turned).

A vampire's stereotypical obsession with physical graces does not preclude his or her need for stimulation in other areas; as they say, beauty is only skindeep. Vivacity and enthusiasm, varied intellectual pursuits, and an earthy worldliness go far in charming most vampires. A sharp and sparkling wit will lend to romantic longevity more than a mathematically flawless face or stunning figure. Your beauty may attract a vampire, but the only way you will keep his or her interest is if you have something more to offer.

On the Prowl: Where to Find Your Future Mate

Battle not with monsters
lest ye become a monster
and if you gaze into the abyss
the abyss gazes into you.
—Friedrich Nietzsche

Even though it seems incredibly logical that the best place to meet a vampire might be a crypt, it is probably the last place you would ever look for one. Vampires are as diverse as humans, and their interests range far and wide. Like most night people, vampires out and about where humans gather: clubs, entertainment events, public transportation depots, etc. In fact, it might just be easier to list all the places you aren't likely to meet a vampire.

It is commonly believed that vampires frequent goth clubs. This is only partially true. Many vampires are amused by the veneration their kind receive among spooky kids, while some are outright offended by it, particularly by the propensity of some clubgoers to emulate vampire stereotypes through their behavior and dress. You are taking a risk in seeking out a vampire mate in this environment, and you will certainly be competing with every other vampire-loving human in the building. In a pinch, it's worth a shot, but most vampires of our acquaintance see goth clubs and bars more as hunting grounds than anything else. As with human dating, the bar scene is best reserved for one-night stands, as that is likely the best you can hope for. But be careful—that one night could be your last.

Our first suggestion for finding a true vampire relationship is simple: When seeking out any mate, human, vampire, or otherwise, it's good to start by exploring opportunities with those who share your same interests—just make sure the events you attend occur after dusk. If you are an avid reader, join nighttime book clubs. If you are the sporting type, attend evening games or participate in competitive sports that take place after sunset. If you are a patron of the arts, seek out nighttime gallery events, concerts, and theatre productions. None of these suggestions will ensure that you will find a vampire, but if you want to have common interests from the start, patience is the key.

When looking for spots to meet your vampire, consider the likelihood that he would find a human to easily feed on there. Human food establishments, in general, should be at the bottom of your list. Odds are that you will not meet a vampire in the grocery store. For one thing, he doesn't need groceries. He has a better pick of feeder humans at other places, and the fluorescent lights in the supermarket are particularly unflattering to vampire complexions. The same goes for most restaurants, unless they become nightclubs later in the evening, in which case you have a shot at finding a vampire there.

Although it might seem a likely place to meet a vampire, it's probably be a safe bet that you would not find one in a prison. Since he or she could just walk out of the cell, using their guile or their strength, a vampire probably would not stay long even if he had allowed himself to be arrested so that he could feed on an unattended prisoner. A funeral home is a bad choice, as a vampire still needs his blood red and blooming, and some vampires find reminders of human mortality to be distasteful. Hell only knows what would happen if he were to drink from the veins of an embalmed corpse. A hospital may be a better bet, as there are comatose patients and ready blood supplies just hanging like fruit ripe for the picking.

If you're looking for a date on public transportation, only a train offers a real eat-and-hide opportunity. A plane is too confined and offers no real escape. Sure, vampires may be able to shift into bat form, but getting sucked (no pun intended) into a jet engine at 30,000 feet is no treat, even for them. Since vampires have the instinct to be secretive, sporting events, where the crowd is concentrating on something else may prove to be choice locations for meeting your vampire.

In general, vampires do enjoy places where the public gathers—all vampires are not recluses. In most metropolitan cities all over the globe, community centers are opening up for vampires as places where they can discuss common political issues and social interests with one another. These community centers often hold public events and gatherings geared at promoting awareness and acceptance of *Homo striga* while developing a sense of kinship among these often solitary individuals. Generally, humans are welcome at most events. The passionate activism of these community centers coupled with society's advances with regards to the rights and realities of vampirism in the general populace is making itself evident in many ways.

Since the advent of the Internet, many online dating services geared toward vampires and those who love them have sprung up. Using personals ads was once seen as an act of desperation, but in recent years, it has become an increasingly acceptable method of meeting potential mates. You run the risk of the same dangers as with human-to-human dating services, but we have found that in reality, humans are more predatory in nature, emotionally and literally, than your average vampire, and vampires, relieved at no longer having to hide their true natures, tend to be more upfront and honest than humans when utilizing this medium. After all, the people who are looking for mates through these online services are obviously open-minded and accepting of vamps!

On most vampire dating websites, the decade in which a vampire was turned is openly listed. This helps preempt many potential problems detailed elsewhere in this book, because you know ahead of time where and when your vampire hails from and whether the residual quirks they may possess from having lived in a specific time period are things you can handle. Most of these dating services also enable you to discuss ahead of time what you are looking for in a mate. Do you only want the pleasures associated with the feeding process, or are you looking for long-term love? Is the vampire seeking thralls, food, friendship, or romance? While this takes some of the mystery out of the romance, it compensates by curtailing issues with miscommunication before they begin. These websites also make it easier for vampires on a practical level, as you can list your blood type.

There are also now human-operated bars, dance clubs, religious institutions, and retail outlets that not only openly proclaim their support of vampires but also cater to the needs of the vampire population. Many stores and service businesses in major cities now offer two sets of operating hours: standard daytime hours for humans, and late night hours for our nocturnal brothers and sisters. Some restaurants have begun catering to a vampire's narrow dietary needs by offering fresh blood from several different types of animals. All of these events and locations make for great options for finding prospective mates.

If all else fails, in New York, Los Angeles, Chicago, Boston, New Orleans, London, and Madrid, vampire-human speed dating is all the rage. A short chat and a quick bite, and you know if you are at least superficially compatible!

Should I Bug Renfield about an Introduction?

Am I not destroying my enemies when I make friends of them?
—Abraham Lincoln

The name Renfield, in association with Bram Stoker's *Dracula* or vampires in general, has come to represent a sort of generic term for "servant" or "friend who serves." You may need an intercessor of some sort, your own Renfield, to meet the vampire of your dreams. Let us take a moment to see where the word "Renfield" comes from.

At the beginning of *Dracula*, R. N. Renfield is confined to a lunatic asylum, although the reader has no idea why. But by the way he acts, the reader knows he is a certifiable loony. He is zoophagous (life-eating) and consumes bugs as a regular course of habit. After a couple attempts to escape from the asylum, he suc-

ceeds. In the book and films, although Renfield pro-
claims his undying devotion to "the master," Dracula
ends up killing him. Always a friend, the term "Renfield" has come to mean someone who will stand by a
dark presence until the very end. In most cases, this is
a vampire's thrall.

In dealing with the question of whether you should
bug your Renfield, the devoted follower of the vampire
you have your sights set on, for an introduction, there
is no simple answer. The relationship between a vampire and his thralls, or attendants, can be a murky
one. It helps to begin by addressing the nature of the
particular thrall and the essence of your vampire's
bond with all his subordinates. Thralls are under a
mild (though in some cases acute) state of hypnosis.
The process by which a vampire binds a thrall to him
is psychochemical and leaves the subject of the procedure in a state of slightly soporific willing subjuga-
tion. The fortitude, wit, and physical strength of the
thrall affect the depth of hypnosis. Some thralls retain
almost all of their previous autonomy, while some
unfortunate individuals have been reduced to raving
lunatics by the procedure due to imbalances caused by
a poor reaction to the effects of the vampire's blood as
it alters their neurochemistry.

In any case, once a thrall has been infused with
the vampire's blood, he or she is bound, psychologically and physically, to the creature. The end result is
a near-slavish devotion to the safety, protection, and

well-being of the vampire. This may or may not act in your favor if you use a thrall to meet his master.

Usually, vampires value their henchmen. They are treated like beloved pets and prizes, and sometimes, in rare cases, the vampires look fondly upon their thralls as charming children. On the other end of the spectrum, some vampires treat their thralls like slaves or fodder. In either case, it is of the utmost importance that you impress upon the thrall that you only have the vampire's best interests at heart. Even if a vampire does not necessarily respect the opinions of their retainers, it is vital that you convince the thrall that you are not a threat to the well-being of their master, or you may find yourself in a precarious and dangerous position. If you make an unfavorable impression, you will likely be cock-blocked, at best, or at worst, attacked.

If you find you need a thrall to get you the introduction to the vampire you so strongly desire, be very cautious, as they will pay no attention to the things that may get you in trouble since the thrall has no perception of his own safety or the safety of others. Keep your eyes open and always be on your guard. He knows the vampire better than you do, and he may just be leading you into a pen to be the next vampire meal.

Befriend the vampire's thralls and show them kindness. Unless you have another way to connect with the vampire of your dreams, your only entrance into the world of the undead may lie within the grasp of this nerdy servant who seems to have no life. Sometimes it is good to have friends in low places.

No Matter What, Am I Too Young for Him?

*The dead might as well try to speak to the living
as the old to the young.*
—Willa Cather

It isn't impossible to cultivate a relationship with a vampire, but it is challenging. One of the primary points of conflict lies in the age difference. It can be difficult enough for humans that are a generation apart to find common ground; the difficulty is compounded exponentially when the gulf is centuries wide.

Dating a fledgling vampire also poses a set of challenges. The transformation from *Homo sapiens* to *Homo striga* can be extremely traumatic, and adjusting to the colossal physical, psychological, and social changes that accompany the transition take time. An individual that possesses a strong personality, or a great deal of wisdom, character, and verve, will usually have a smoother transformation than someone with a weak spirit. If you are a nurturing individual, you may be able to play a part in helping a young vampire adjust to his new life, but the role of caretaker is not right for everyone.

Is the vampire of your dreams a new vampire or an elder? If he is an elder, although he may be youthful in appearance, there is really no choice here for you or him—it just won't work. Everyone he meets is like a child in their knowledge base compared to his. You can't compete. You can't read the encyclopedia to catch up on centuries' worth of information (or watch the film, for those of you waiting for that event). You can't bluff your way through this. His only peers are other elders who, like himself, have existed for centuries. Our one bit of advice in this case is *stay away*. The two of you would be a deadly combination. You would no more want to date him than you would your grandfather. Even if he did not treat you like feeder cattle, your conversations would be as dull as dishwater. His priorities and needs are often dramatically different from a human's, and sometimes this causes difficulties in seeing eye-to-eye. Finding a compatible temperament and sharing a worldview is key, no matter how many hundreds of years separate your birthdays. We would advise against relationships with elder vampires, but if you insist, use extreme caution.

A fledgling vampire is a different story. He or she will be closer to your age, give or take a century. You need to have some sort of age or ideology equality to spark a vampire's interest. He needs for you to be able to relate to his likes and dislikes. If a vampire was turned in 1920s America, and was the sort that loved a free and easy lifestyle, frequenting speakeasies and drinking the night away, and you are a twenty-first century party-going club kid that loves dancing and bar hopping until dawn, you will likely find yourselves very compatible.

No matter what age vampire you date, the real trick is to find the common bond between the two of you. Dig out his interests during conversation and then exploit them for your own gain within the relationship. If you are the contemplative, introspective sort with a love for philosophy and witty discourse, you may find true love with a vampire from ancient Athens, while a Spartan vampire would make an excellent mate for a modern Navy SEAL. If you want to share your life with a "traditional" gentleman or lady, seek out Victorian vampires. If decadence and debauchery light your fire, you can quench your lusts with a pre-revolutionary French aristocrat or a former follower of Paculla Annia, the notorious Roman priestess who made many reforms to the Bacchanalia, expanding the range of its indulgence and including all—women and men, young and old, free men and slaves—in a monthly five-day-long celebration of the ecstasy of wine, sex, and madness. It is not difficult to find someone whose needs and desires match your own. Again, patience is integral.

Another point to be aware of is to never, ever discuss your age or his. It will only make him more aware of your differences and start him thinking about just how temporary (at least through the eyes of his lifespan) your relationship will be. Keep the conversation away from age, and anytime you feel it slip in that direction, quickly intercede with something upbeat to distract him. Of course, you could always intervene with your main distraction—you. But you may want to save playing that trump card for the worst of times when nothing else will get his mind out of those places you do not want it to be in.

The best advice we have is to use the same criteria you would for dating mere mortals. Even though it is easier to tell ages with humans, you have to find out whom and what exactly you are dealing with in terms of your vampire quarry and then simply use a little common sense. However, your charms may be your greatest asset and your easiest entrance into his inner circle. But even your charming ways will not excite him forever, so be sure you make good use of "pillow talk" to unzip his personality, reach inside, and pull out his personal interests.

To Play It Safe, Should My First Date Be a Double?

> One of the saddest lessons of history is this:
> If we've been bamboozled long enough, we tend to reject any
> evidence of the bamboozle. The bamboozle has captured us.
> Once you give a charlatan power over you,
> you almost never get it back. —Carl Sagan

You have met your vampire in a public place or at a social gathering, such as a club, theatre, a friend's house, or, just by dumb luck, at the blood bank. You have spent enough time with him to feel somewhat safe in his presence. You want to go out on a date with him alone.

ARE YOU NUTS?

It is going to take time before you can begin to ascertain whether he is being charming and gracious because he is enamored of you, or if he is buttering you up for his feast. We aren't speaking ill of vampires; these are cold, hard facts. After all, you're reading this to find out how to date a vampire, and we have spent a lot of time with them. You should take all of the intelligent precautions you would in dating anyone you have just met, human or vampire.

Some would say that it is always best to go on double dates when you first start seeing someone new. Going out in a group can soften the awkwardness of being with a new person, particularly if you are a little shy, and when your prospective mate is a vampire, a group can lend a sense of additional security. The latter is true even if your date is human; you never know if a pretty face and charming demeanor are masking sinister intentions. With vampires, you should figure it like this: If someone was a real asshole in life, then they will usually be an even bigger one after they've turned. If someone was a thief and smuggler in their human incarnation, then you cannot expect them to suddenly become enlightened and much more loaded with moral fiber as a vampire. Do you get it? Some vampires transcend the crimes and frailties of their mortal lives, and some rise above the brutality of their vampiric existence, but it is a rough road to travel, and it takes willing introspection and a vast reservoir of strength to be able to change for the better.

What we are trying to encourage is the use of common sense. Unfortunately, it will be harder for you to use common sense with a vampire than with a human. You have a lot of things working against you: the vampire's supernatural charm, his knowledge base from centuries of accumulated information, his need for blood to sustain himself, his hypnotic grace and elegance, and his ability to completely sweep you off your feet and take you off on an eternal romantic relationship. It would be very easy for you to get caught up in his psychological embrace. Stop! He is a charmer, yes, but you need to keep some distance between you and his smoldering personality. The more recently you've met him, the greater that distance needs to be, psychologically speaking.

Who you will take with you on this double date is a very important choice. You need a trusted friend, a confidante, whom you can bounce ideas off. You don't want to bring anyone who is closed-minded, and it goes without saying that you should absolutely refrain from bringing any friend who may have negative feelings about vampires. Their animosity or fear would certainly taint the date from the start, unless you bring them along as a free snack for your date.

It is best to bring along an easygoing, sociable couple that possess a warm, passionate chemistry with one another, and it would be best if it were a couple with a strong, loving relationship. It can only help to have an example of a good interpersonal connection along with you on a first date. Keep everything as light and positive as possible. Upbeat, friendly people are naturally buoyant, and will help you through any awkward moments. You want someone not to encourage you and to be a cheerleader, but someone who has more mental distance from your vampire than you do. You need to listen to your friend, and every time you two have opposing ideas about the date, you should stop and talk them out.

The downside of a group or double date is that it cuts down on opportunities for intimacy, both sexual and psychological, but you don't want to invite too much intimacy, on that first date, or even the next few that follow. Remember to go slow: You may meet the vampire of your dreams, but you may also just meet a charming, bloodsucking killer who would like nothing more than to take you to a bed that you would never leave. Patience is the most valuable commodity in this case. After all, if you are working on a relationship that will last an eternity, what is a little extra time in making sure you are safe and not sorry?

Can We Only Meet at Night?

When one is in love, one always begins by deceiving one's self,
and one always ends by deceiving others.
That is what the world calls a romance.
—Oscar Wilde, *The Picture of Dorian Gray*

Meeting your date at night brings with it an entire emotional and psychological stigma that may or may not be correct. Night is the great concealer. It is a place to hide, away from the sun, away from the revealing light of daytime and scrutiny. If you're hesitant about meeting your vampire at night, could it be that you don't want to feel you have something to hide? Or is it because you have classes or a day job that make it impossible to be awake all night? We again come to one of the central dilemmas of dating a vampire: Do you adjust to him or does he adjust to you? A schedule of when both of you are going to be awake and able to be with one another is only one small hair on the entire rat of your relationship.

As was previously discussed, the vampire's choice to avoid sunlight is not an aesthetic one, and it is not a matter of preference: for vampires, solar radiation causes illness, injury, and in some cases, death. For this reason, vampires avoid exposure to sunlight as much as possible, and they are very scheduled beings due to their survival instincts.

But there are some experts who believe that the entire "vampires can only go out at night" idea is a myth in itself. Scientists have been experimenting with topical sunblock that will protect a vampire from the adverse effects of sunlight, but as of this writing, none of these experiments has come to complete fruition. The rising sun does not instantaneously render a vampire comatose, so they can function normally during daylight hours as long as they stay indoors and away from sunlight, particularly the sun's ultraviolet rays. Remember that even Christopher Lee's Dracula was fine in the daylight until that schmuck Van Helsing, played by Peter Cushing, tore down the curtains, letting in the sunlight.

Many fiction authors have assumed that the vampires they write about are quite capable of existing in the daytime. Such classics as Nancy A. Collins's *Sunglasses After Dark*, Nancy Baker's *A Terrible Beauty*, and Chelsea Quinn Yarbro's Count Saint Germaine series make no bones about their heroes walking around in the daylight, although they usually have some minor protections, such as sunblock and dark glasses. The general consensus seems to be that the vampire's powers are considerably diminished during the daylight hours. They fall into a trance or coma but can be easily awakened if they are disturbed. Even though they are weakened in this state, they are still stronger and more powerful than a normal human. This should serve as a warning to all ill-educated vampire hunters.

It has been said, however, that some of the older and more powerful vampires do not need this daytime coma. If you are dating one of these, you may be able to meet discreetly during daylight hours. But your vampire will always be much more comfortable venturing forth from the sanctuary of his or her lair in the evening, and you shouldn't expect a vampire to meet with you, even in the safety of a secure building, during daytime hours until you have established a very strong bond of trust.

Dining Out: Is It a Date Option?

> *What is food to one, is to others bitter poison.*
> —Lucretius, *De Rerum Natura*

Variety is the spice of life, and we don't just mean sexually (although that isn't a bad idea either). We mean you need to mix it up, get out, go places, and see things. But you are dating a vampire, and that does affect the type of dates the two of you can go on.

Going out to dinner at a restaurant is usually a traditional option for run-of-the-mill, human-to-human dates. But given a vampire's dietary needs, this usually safe choice of venue becomes a bit more complicated. Dining out is all right, but you need to carefully consider your date location. For example, a nice restaurant often has a dark and moody atmosphere. That should, at the very least, make him feel a little more secure than, say, a brightly lit skating rink in midtown Manhattan would.

Generally, vampires have no interest in restaurants, though some do evidence a small interest in gastronomy and may have fond memories of cuisine related to their country of origin. Dining out, to a vampire, takes on a very different meaning within their unique cultural and biological context. Some may enjoy the people-watching aspect of this sort of date, but if you truly want a shared experience, obviously dining out should not be your first choice. You are essentially inviting your prospective mate to an event where they cannot be a participant, and are only spectators. Until you and your mate are closer and you are able to discern whether accompanying you while you eat is something they might enjoy, it is best to endeavor to find activities that you can both appreciate.

Many older vampires have made an effort to blend into human society and are more comfortable in restaurants. Transeo, in particular, are extremely skilled at mimicking the act of eating as a human does, passing even under the most intense scrutiny. All of our Transeo friends and associates usually possess flawless table manners and dining etiquette that would put etiquette expert Letitia Baldrige to shame. For most younger vampires, however, the scent of food cooking, especially heavier, more savory dishes, can be nausea inducing. If your vampire has been turned within the last few decades, it is not wise to invite him or her to a restaurant at all. The social discomfort combined with the physical discomfort is a recipe for disaster.

In general, vampires feed alone. They prefer solitude during the hunt, as it is both a sensual and necessary process, and the presence of a human during the hunt is almost certainly both dangerous and indiscreet. This changes if they are planning on passing on their condition to a human. In this case, they usually bring their protégé along with them for the purposes of instruction and elucidation. Occasionally, however, a vampire will bring a human mate along on a hunt as part of a deeper bonding experience and as a way to establish trust and a more profound understanding. This is very meaningful, but it can be incredibly shocking for the human. Whatever your preconceived romantic notions may be about vampires feeding, it is in reality a brutal act and is not something that many humans can witness without being shaken to the core.

The really basic questions to ask yourself here are: (a) Are we going out at night? In most cases the answer will be yes; (b) Will he feel secure where we are going? A darkened restaurant can feel as secure as a large crowd event. Just plan out your seating, keeping comfort and convenient exits in mind; (c) Are his thoughts going to be on me or his next feeding? When did he last feed and will the other people at the venue become a distraction to him? A little common sense can go a long way toward making your nights out together pleasing and worthwhile. Plan ahead and you really should not have any trouble.

Should I Be Talkative or Deadly Silent?

*A well bred woman may easily and effectually promote
the most useful and elegant conversation without speaking
a word. The modes of speech are scarcely more variable
than the modes of silence.* —Tom Blair

Think of conversation as a pendulum. It swings in two directions, back and forth, to and fro. The extreme end of a swing in either direction is too extreme. Talking too much or not talking at all are both wrong ways to approach your vampire. This is, in many ways, no different from dating humans. Think about it. How would you like someone you meet for the first time to behave? Do you want to have to draw conversation out of them, or would you like them to dominate every moment with talking? Your answer is probably neither.

Listen to yourself in the conversation. If you feel you are over-talking (a good indication is the use of a lot of run-on sentences and double-talk, or a sudden lack of input from him) just stop, take a break, and very politely excuse yourself for a moment. You can always use the powder room as a reason to break away. When you return, it will be like a fresh start. You do not want him to see you suffer from what is referred to as "The Oprah Complex" or the "ICARE Complex," which stands for:

Inclusion   You are talking too much because you need someone to talk to and want to be included in every person's plan. The stench of desperation will follow you around the room.

Control   You are talking too much because you want someone to do something for you. But he's not ready, yet, for you to ask him for a favor.

Affection   You are talking too much because you want everyone to know that you care. Let your natural conversation show that instead of pushing.

Relaxation   You are talking too much because talking allows you to relax and unwind. The problem is that it may make everybody else around you nervous and uptight.

Escape   You are talking too much because you're trying to put off something else you should be doing. Go do it and quit making a fool of yourself.

Vampires have as many different personalities as humans do. They were once people. Not every human will like the same thing. Not every vampire will like the same thing. But there are general rules of thumb to fall back upon when you are unsure of your demeanor. Most people who talk too much do so because they are nervous or ill at ease. This is normal for the first time you actually meet your vampire. You will be in a new and very uncomfortable situation and are bound to be a little nervous. Take a moment before you speak. Remember that he will almost always be attracted to the same thing you are: someone who is confident and self-assured.

When you first meet someone, be it a vampire, human, or anyone else, it is a good idea to avoid conversing about certain topics altogether, namely politics, religion, and personal finance. The latter is rough terrain and best avoided. Vampires, due to their extended lifespans, are generally very well-off. You absolutely do not want to give the impression that you are a gold digger or *grave digger*, as such opportunists are known in vampire parlance. The first two can very easily become points of contention, even under the best of circumstances. Politics and religion are naturally heated topics that people, and vampires, can be very passionate and emotional about, and it is easy to butt heads very quickly over religious concepts or political points of view.

Contrary to many self-help manuals, you really should not spend any time preparing or figuring out ahead of time what it is you want to say. Your conversation will end up coming out stilted and you will feel a little foolish. Instead, stay cool and just listen. After your introduction to him, listen to what the vampire says first. Follow his thoughts as a lead-in to the conversation. Let your natural personality come forward and trust yourself. Please, no bobbing your head and agreeing with every word like an airhead. When it is appropriate, show him that you have your own interests and that you keep up with current events. Over time, and as he listens to your responses, his natural interests will come forth and so will yours. It is only when you find out who the real vampire is inside that he will become truly attractive. This will work the same way for him.

It is considered to be in extremely poor taste to inquire about the events surrounding a vampire's turning, and this is something that they generally do not discuss with someone at all until they feel as though they can trust the person implicitly. It is not that the tale of their turning is some sort of Achilles' heel that exposes an exploitable vulnerability; it is simply a deeply personal subject for most vampires, and not something to be broached lightly. It can be kind of like talking to your grandfather about the war.

Death is a difficult subject for humans to discuss, and this is even truer with vampires. Generally, talking about death either brings to mind the challenges and stigmas they face with regards to their dietary needs or conjures up memories of loved ones they have lost throughout the ages. Feelings about this are bad and bad.

To a lesser degree, avoid bringing up exes. Do you really want to hear tales that span centuries upon centuries about your date's romances? Do you truly want to hear about his one night stand with a barbarian wench in Carthage or his liaison with an Olmec priestess? No matter how honest we think we want to be with prospective mates from the start, the truth of the matter is that some information is best divulged later in a relationship, if ever. He does not want to know about the experimenting you did in college or the ex that you dumped because he didn't change the toilet paper roll when it was finished, and you don't want to know about the wacky weekend your vampire beau spent cavorting with grape-besotted revelers before a Bacchus festival in 350 BC (trust us, you really don't want to know).

To know when to communicate and when to stop is a one of the most important traits a person can cultivate within themselves. AMOC (Automated Mouth Overload Control) can become deadly if it is faulty. It can stop your future plans before they even get started. Take a good look at yourself and see if you may need to practice restraint.

Je Ne Sais Quoi: Adding a Little Mystery to Your Humanity

Now comes the mystery.
—Henry Ward Beecher, last words, March 8, 1887

Mystery is a very important element in any scheme of dating, but it is more so when you are dating somebody who has *seen it all* and *done it all*. When you see those gifts or advertisements that state "for the man who has everything," they are really talking about your vampire. Remember that even in a human-to-human relationship, playing games is a bad idea, but when you attempt to play relationship games with a vampire, it could be deadly. It's unlikely that conventional romance games and petty manipulations will go unnoticed, and it's extremely unlikely that they will work.

To create intrigue or mystery in his eyes and stir up your dating life is going to take a massive effort on your part and require all of your wiles. It is difficult for a human to put on an air of drama and inscrutability that will effectively intrigue a vampire. The mystery that you would want to truly cultivate cannot be full of false airs and melodramatics. Your beauty lies within your humanity. It is the one thing he does not posses, and being genuine and down-to-earth will score you far more points than falsities will. You are going to have to work much harder than you did in meeting him, because what you are trying to do now is set him up for the long run. Nobody is going to stick around for decades with someone who bores them. Mystery is never boring.

While it is believed that Pierre Choderlos de Laclos's epistolary novel *Les Liaisons Dangereuses* is a work of fiction written to expose the decadence and perversity of France's ancien régime, it is actually a story rooted in truth. It is loosely based on letters that illustrated some of the complex emotional puppetry of a Tombeur called, at the time, by the name of the Marquise de Louvel. She was a *noblesse de robe* by way of purchased title and, secretly, a vampire that hailed from the time of Charlemagne. While the villain of de Laclos's tale meets a poetically just social demise, her real-life counterpart not only survived, but prospered. De Louvel's victims were, in reality, destroyed to a one, and when their suffering could no longer provide the Marquise with amusement, they were drained until death. Clearly, in such an unlevel romantic playing field, it is best not to play at all.

The phrase *je ne sais quoi* literally means "I don't know what." But most often it is used in terms of a quality, as in "I don't know what it is about her, but she has something special." What she has is je ne sais quoi, or the "it" factor. Some people are born with it, and some manufacture it. Since you cannot be born with enough mystery to intrigue a vampire, your job is to produce it, smother yourself with it, and make it look very natural, very real. It is a positive thing to have that mysterious something about you. It is an alluring factor that one finds hard to put into words. Some of you will not be able to cultivate it at all.

But how do you give yourself that unknown or indescribable quality that will really make him stop and take notice? It is actually a combination of things, all of which take patience and timing. You should also refer back to the chapter entitled "Should I Be Talkative or Deadly Silent?" (page 117). Couple your speech patterns with the way you look at him—flatter him with your eyes, but make it always seem as if you are keeping a secret about yourself or what you think of him. Always make him feel as if you are holding onto emotional information that he will have to work to get out of you. You are the secret itself, and he must *never* know everything about you.

Prowling Pompeii: How Much Do You Really Need to Know about His History?

*As we know, there are known knowns; there are things we
know we know. We also know there are known unknowns;
that is to say we know there are some things we do not know.
But there are also unknown unknowns—the ones we don't know
we don't know.* —Donald H. Rumsfeld,
Department of Defense news briefing

Let's say you're dating a guy who was not only in the
Marines, but was stationed overseas in wartime. Do
you grill him about his service record without knowing anything about either the Marines or the war? Or

what if you're dating a lovely lady who was a nurse that helped in the rescue and recovery efforts from the Indonesian tsunami. Do you grill her about all the bloody details while knowing absolutely nothing about either tsunamis or Indonesia, or do you do a little basic research on either or both before that comes up as dinner conversation?

Possessing a familiarity with your vampire's heritage, their timeline, and the historical and cultural path that he or she has tread is not only useful but often vital if you want to have any hope of a lasting relationship or true understanding. Showing an interest in your vampire's life and unlife shows that you care for them and that you are willing to take steps to bring the two of you closer. What experiences shaped this vampire? What occupations did he or she hold? Was your vampire a politician? Warrior? Homemaker? Teacher or philosopher? What societal caste did they belong to (this question seems irrelevant in our day and age, but was historically of utmost importance)? What were the gender expectations of their time? What were the pivotal historical events that they lived through, and how involved were they in these events? What experienced did they have during these vastly different periods of their existence? Take the time to learn about your vampire, and then research as much relevant historical and sociological background as you can.

The way you answer the questions above will have a lot to do with the way you will approach the question, How much do you really need to know about his history? In one respect, no one really likes to be questioned as if they are in the middle of a journalistic interview. Many times, people do not want to talk about atrocities they have witnessed, wars they have waged, or catastrophes that they experienced. But in a relationship, those things tend to come out over time, not only because you would naturally ask about them now and then, but also because it is cathartic and liberating to be able to share those things and get them off of your chest in a safe and loving environment.

Most vampires are extremely nostalgic about their human lives, even if they are loath to admit it. They have a deeply rooted sentimentality for a time when things were simpler for them; the complexities of life are rarely as tortuous as those of undeath. Vampires will also often harbor strong feelings, both positive and negative, about the many eras that they lived through and the countries that they stalked.

As we have said time and time again, most vampires have *seen it all* and have probably *done it all.* That does not mean that they don't want to enjoy the energizing and beneficial properties that come from sharing a traumatic moment from their past with a loved one. However, there are some don'ts here. Number one is *do not interrogate him about past survival kills.* Feel him out and *do not push.* And *never remind him of the fact that you are not equals.* Educating yourself about the times and places in which your vampire has existed can help you prevent any potentially uncomfortable faux pas and bungles that may be fatal to the relationship.

But be cautious: A little knowledge can be a dangerous thing. Make sure that you do not go into this half-cocked. If you are going to delve into this level of research on your vampire, do it thoroughly, and beware of glibly tossing out historically inaccurate nonsense. You also need to be conscious of personal nuances. Are there bad memories attached to a particular time period? Purchasing a Qing Dynasty vase to decorate your new apartment will not impress a vampire that was defeated in the Battle of Ningyuan in 1626. Discussing the imprisonment of Mary Stuart may accidentally remind your vampire of a romance that ended poorly in 1567. Share his experiences and turn them around to so he begins to almost depend on you for emotional healing.

I Think He Can See Right through Me— Do I Need Make-up?

> *Avoiding danger is no safer in the long run*
> *than outright exposure.* —Helen Keller

In the Twilight series, created by Stephenie Meyer, 107-year-old sensitive, whiny, emo "teen" vampire Edward is the heartthrob who can read minds. In Twilight's *New Moon*, there is a mind-reading vampire by the name of Aro. Count Dracula displayed telepathic and mind-control abilities. He could even hypnotize or mesmerize his victims.

True psychic vampires are said to possess and control great telepathic abilities. But does that mean they can actually mind reads? Can all vampires read minds? What exactly is mind-reading? Are mind-reading and telepathy the same thing?

Let us do a little definition delving here. Mind-control goes by a variety of names, such as brain-washing or thought reform. You do not have to be a vampire or have supernatural abilities to be able to succeed at mind-control. You just need a victim whom you are able to break down by any variety of means, such as sleep deprivation or solitary confinement. Once the victim's mind is a clean slate, you can write anything on it that you would like.

We have previously discussed the importance of the thrall in vampire culture. Taken literally, *thrall* means "to enslave." That can be a physical or an intellectual enslavement. It can be a form of mind-control that forces someone to do the controller's bidding, as illustrated in the relationship of the Count and Renfield in Bram Stoker's *Dracula*. This is the ultimate submission: A vampire's thrall is addicted to both the blood and the personality of the vampire, and through this addiction, the thrall relinquishes all control to their vampire. If you were to succumb to your vampire in this way, you would lose your ability to think for yourself, and would be almost entirely at your vampire's bidding. But then, that may be what you desire.

Mind-reading, on the other hand, is a para-psychological ability wherein someone uses their mind to tap into your mind's wavelengths and can understand what you are thinking. This is very, very rare. If you suspect your vampire is reading your thoughts, remember that mind-reading tricks are a dime a dozen. It is much more likely that you are being swindled or deluded than actually having your mind read.

In other words, no, a vampire cannot read minds. His or her seeming ability to do so stems from eons of experience in reading people and experiencing both human and vampire machinations.

Better Haunts & Gravestones: How to Make Your Home Hospitable

*This is the true nature of home—it is the place of Peace;
the shelter, not only from injury, but from all terror,
doubt and division.* —John Ruskin

Home is more than shelter from the elements; it is a sanctuary. It is the womb in which we live, that place we have all been trying to crawl back into ever since we were born. It is the container of harmony and tranquility. It is where you can turn off and just be you, that person who has been zipped inside of your skin all day.

Now imagine that those hours have actually been decades. Imagine you've spent them on the run, always looking behind you or around every corner for trouble. You have created problems, and now you must run from them. To finally escape is to be home.

If you want to take your relationship to the next, more intimate, level, providing a safe, well-protected, sun-proofed haven for your mate goes a very long way toward establishing trust and a foundation for a long-term relationship. If your living area cannot accommodate this type of shelter, it is unlikely that your vampire will ever be able to spend the night. If you plan on eventually cohabitating with a vampire, these are all important points to consider. Moving in with a vampire is a very important step and is not something that should be taken lightly. His or her needs with regards to privacy and safety will not have to take precedence over your needs as a matter of survival.

* * *

Our ways are not your ways,
and there shall be to you many strange things.
—Count Dracula, *Dracula*, Bram Stoker

* * *

Your home's décor is of little importance. Be yourself. It does not matter if you fancy the rich colors and exotic feel of Moroccan decoration, or if your house is filled with Neofuturist clear acrylic furniture like a scene from *Logan's Run*. If retro '70s avocado-green linoleum is your thing and there are pink flamingos in your yard, no problem. If it fits your tastes, keep it. To make your vampire comfortable in your home, there is no need to invest in or even re-create a coffin, paint the walls blood red, fill the candelabras with black tapers, drape the windows with heavy swaths of velvet, and have Berlioz's *Symphonie fantastique* playing in the background—unless, of course, that's your preferred aesthetic. Not all vampires have the same tastes, and no matter who you are attempting to cultivate a relationship with, human or vampire, you want them to love you for who you are and not something you are pretending to be. If you are comfortable with yourself, your companion will be comfortable with you.

* * *

How blessed are some people, whose lives have no fears, no dreads, to whom sleep is a blessing that comes nightly, and brings nothing but sweet dreams.
—Lucy Westenra, *Dracula*, Bram Stoker

* * *

Ensuring your vampire's physical comfort of your vampire is fairly straightforward. If he or she is overnighting, you must be able to provide sanctuary from the ill effects of sunlight. During daylight hours, a vampire must rest in a room or other enclosure that is completely protected from any solar radiation, direct or indirect sunlight. It is best if this room can be locked from the inside to offer a stronger sense of security and soundproofed against the cacophony of everyday human daytime activities. No one wants to be woken from a dead sleep by a leaf blower or clanging trash truck. Security is of the utmost importance, especially considering a vampire's relative vulnerability during these hours and the very valid concerns they have over personal safety after a millennium of persecution.

When younger vampires first wake, they are generally famished. Put aside your Mediterranean cookbooks when your mate is visiting, as the scent of garlic is offensive to vampires. It's not injurious, but they do find it nauseating. It goes without saying: You do not want to make your mate queasy.

You can't expect a vampire, especially one that is less than two or three hundred years old, to stick around after they wake. It's nothing personal; their need for blood nourishment is simply more urgent than their elder brothers' and sisters', and they usually have the need to feed right away. Generally, vampires must consume approximately 7 percent of their body weight in blood roughly every 72 hours, and the older a vampire is, the longer they can exist without blood intake.

Synthetic blood is now coming on the market, and in time you may find it prudent to purchase some to keep in your house for vampire guests, but at the time of this writing, there are none that provide the nourishment or psychological satisfaction of fresh blood.

Your job is to make your abode hospitable for

your vampire, that is, to make it warm, friendly, and comfortable. It needs to be a place where a deep breath and a heavy sigh signals the end of all the night's travails before he ventures out again. He *must* leave and he *must* desire to come back. If you want him, it is your job to make him want to come back home to you.

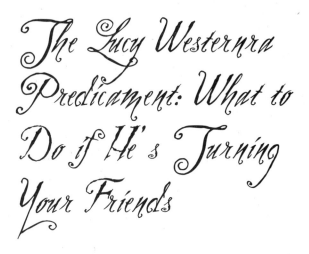

The Lucy Westenra Predicament: What to Do if He's Turning Your Friends

The worst solitude is to be destitute of sincere friendship.
—Sir Francis Bacon

It is hard to not be a little concerned about the possibility that your mate will view your friends as either sources of sustenance or potential thralls. Too many rumors have surrounded vampires for ages. What if your mate decides to turn one of your friends? What does this mean? What do you do?

Betrayal. It is a harsh word, but the reality is that when it comes right down to it, if your vampire starts turning your friends and you could have prevented it from happening and did not, then you have betrayed them. To betray a loving friend can be second in pain and heartache only to forsaking a family member. You try to find ways to explain it. You try to rationalize and justify it by thinking of all the reasons that you are not to blame yourself for this despicable act. But your gut tells you the truth, no matter what your head says.

As we have discussed earlier in this book, a vampire's needs are as complex as his or her relationships, and the inherent differences between *Homo sapiens* and *Homo striga* are sometimes difficult for a human to understand. We have illustrated many instances where it may be up to you, the human, to find common ground or make concessions. Unfortunately, the burden and challenge of flexibility and understanding often falls to the human half of a relationship. However, that does not mean that you always have to compromise or bend, especially on issues that are important to you. As a rule, civilized vampires would never entertain the idea of putting a human mate in the position of choosing their mates over their friends and family, but some vampires have little understanding or memory of human emotional responses.

In most cases, it is a huge sign of disrespect if your vampire mate feeds on your loved ones, and it is a dire breach of confidence if he or she makes them into thralls. This applies even if your friend or family member willingly becomes the vampire's food or devoted servant. It is a matter of trust and consideration, and it is also an issue of shared intimacy.

If this issue arises in your relationship, the decision on what direction to take is entirely in your hands. First off, do your friends know that your new partner is a vampire? This is a big consideration, because if they do, they have the option of distancing themselves from the two of you. If they do not know, are they the type of people who can handle being told that a vampire has entered their social circle? If you cannot tell your friends about your vampire, then you are assuming all the risk, and it is up to you to come up with an alternate plan to get your significant other away from your friends. Even though they need to accept some responsibility if they know his true identity. it is never right to blame the victim.

We by no means take this subject lightly. It is a matter of life and death and must be addressed with the sobriety it requires. Be cautious, and keep your suspicions in check. Nothing turns someone off quite like unjust or unfounded accusations, so do not jump at shadows. If you are concerned that your mate may be preying on humans that are close to you, you need to start a dialogue. It is best if you discuss this delicate issue before it becomes a reality. Make it clear that your find it unacceptable that your friends or family would be prey.

It may all come down to the ultimate decision. Who is more important: your friends of many years or

Beware of Jealousy

I had fallen for a vampire named Galina. She
seemed so kind and gentle, and she was smarter,
funnier, and more interesting than any other
woman I had ever met. We got along great, and
I felt comfortable enough to introduce her to my
family very early on. They're open-minded people,
and I didn't think it was a problem. Sure enough,
she hit it off with my folks and with my brother,
and they were very accepting of her nature. I wish
I had been as unprejudiced as they were, or as
unprejudiced as I thought I was.

I was spending more and more time Galina
when my brother fell ill. At first, I thought my
brother only a cold, but the illness lingered. He
became paler and more listless, had no energy, was
weak, irritable, and sweated all the time. I kept
telling him he needed to go see a doctor, but he was
stubborn, insisting it was mono or something like
that, but I didn't believe him. How many 27-year-
old guys do you know who get mono?

As he grew sicker, I became more and more
suspicious of Galina. I became convinced that she
was bleeding him dry. I wanted to trust her, but

your new vampire? Do you have loyalties and where
are they placed, or are they misplaced? It is, in all
honesty, only a decision that you can make. Will you
make the correct one? You may not even be able to

how could I? She was a freakin' vampire, and no matter how much I thought I loved her, nothing was going to change what she was. My brother's illness persisted, and part of me kept telling myself that he would get better soon and that it was just a prolonged cold or something, or maybe it really was mono. But another part of me was becoming more and more certain that Galina was feeding on him.

This voice in my head kept nagging at me, insisting that Galina was doing this, and one day I just blew up. I accused Galina of preying on my family, of betraying my trust, and of using all of us. She didn't say anything at all, she didn't try to argue with me or defend herself. She just stood there frozen for a moment, sneering at me, and then she left my apartment, smashing my living room window as she went.

A week after that confrontation, my brother was diagnosed with Addison's disease, an adrenal disorder. I realized then that it wasn't Galina's fault. I had never bothered to talk to Galina about it or to look for any actual evidence that she was feeding on him. I just assumed that she was the cause of his sickness because of what she was.

turn to your best friend for advice. She may not be around anymore if she realizes you are dating a vampire. Does that matter to you or not?

Vulnerable, Not Victim: Showing Your Gentler Side

*When we were children, we used to think that when we were
grown-up we would no longer be vulnerable.
But to grow up is to accept vulnerability...
To be alive is to be vulnerable.* —Madeleine L'Engle,
Walking on Water: Reflections on Faith and Art

The word *vulnerable* showed up around the year
1600 and is derived from the Latin word *vulnerabilis*
meaning "woundable." As it has morphed with time,
it has come to mean susceptible to being wounded
or even more importantly, "wounded by criticism,
temptation, or love." To be a complete person within
a relationship, one must be open, and that means you
need to be vulnerable. When you're dating a vampire,

there are even more things to which you can be exposed, and even possible mind controls that you are unaware of but that you will be incapable of putting up a defense against.

There is a lot of trust required in a relationship, unless you create a superficial façade and pretend that you're just having fun and nobody will really get hurt. Is that what you want? Do you want to spend your time pretending to have a relationship? We would assume not, as this is an awful lot of trouble to go through just to be with a vampire and not be serious about the two of you as a couple. Is he just a trophy vampire? Be careful, because if he is and gets wind of it, you may end up being the head on the plaque above his doorway.

Being vulnerable means being difficult to defend. But you do not go into a relationship to defend yourself. You go into a relationship to give yourself away. If you have second thoughts, if you have qualms about being in the relationship, then *walk away*! It's not worth it. You can get hurt, and not just emotionally. Think long and hard about it. But if you are committed to this relationship, you must give yourself to him in order for him to relax enough to trust you. A true relationship is all about giving, and when both parties involved do that it, comes back to them one hundred fold.

Showing your gentler side does not mean you are weak. It means you are real. Weakness implies something or someone who is liable to collapse under stress. But as we have already informed you, a relationship with a vampire is not for the weak of heart. You need to be strong. You need to have fortitude. You need to have love, and you need to be open for this thing to work at all.

While some vampires may have some residual ideas regarding gender stereotypes that have remained imprinted from their time as humans, most vampires do believe in gender equality. In many ways, the conversion to *Homo striga* blurs gender lines. Both male and female vampires are equally strong, equally powerful, and parallel each other perfectly in the hunt. There is no glass ceiling among their kind, and positions of power within their society are not determined by whether a vampire is male or female. Any Victorian gentleman who was turned quickly found that his female peers were not the gentle, submissive shrinking violets he had come to expect, and if he were wise, he would not dare treat a female vampire as a second class citizen or risk peril of his life.

In many ways, your vampire is your peer, but in other areas, they simply eclipse the average human. It is difficult to not feel overwhelmed sometimes when interacting with a person who possesses significantly more physical power than you do and has untold additional years of life experience. A vampire may be of a conflicted mind regarding his or her relationship with a human. A human's fragility and naivety can be strong sources of attraction for a vampire, as are a human's earthiness and the connection they maintain with the stream of current society. However, these traits can also be liabilities, as far as a vampire is concerned.

A human's physical vulnerability and naivety can compel a vampire to feel as though they have been put in the position of protector. This storybook dynamic has appeal to those who value the "knight in shining armor" romance trope, and it can form the basis of a relationship right off the bat. Vampires can be just as nurturing as any other living creature, and being put in a position of protector and provider can help assuage any guilt the vampire feels with regard to their dietary needs. It can be refreshing to act as guardian instead of hunter for a time.

The dramatic highs and lows of this sort of relationship are well-known, but these hierarchal connections are doomed to failure in the long run, especially if the human takes advantage of it. Fairy-tale romance wears off with the last throes of infatuation, and if you want a relationship to last, it has to be one of equals. Obviously, this is a challenge given the vampire's inherent strengths, so it is important to show that you have something to bring to the table, and that you are not going to exploit the support that your vampire mate is capable of providing.

The question is, What do you have to offer? A vampire is extremely vulnerable during daylight hours. Can you provide a sense of safety and protection? Can you assist in taking care of the errands that must be done during the day? Your vampire may have difficulty acclimating to cultural shifts. Can you help your mate develop an understanding of changing times? Can you assist them in understanding human society, and, if he or she so desires, can you assist them in blending in with humans?

Provide a haven, establish trust, and be a true and loyal confidant for your vampire, and you will be well on your way to establishing a relationship of equality.

The Van Helsing Issue: What to Do When Your Friends Disapprove

I thoroughly disapprove of duels. If a man should challenge me,
I would take him kindly and forgivingly by the hand and lead
him to a quiet place and kill him. —Mark Twain

Maybe you spent several of the past years squirreled away studying up on vampires. You surrounded yourself with your own created world and now live in the suffocating cocoon of your own exhaling. You have deemed yourself ready, and you began to frequent clubs, libraries, and other places where you may meet that vampire you've been fanaticizing about all this time. Then, *whamo!*, you meet one, and now you are dating. If this is your scenario, the odds are you don't

Text continued on page 156.

Who Was Van Helsing?

Bram Stoker's vampire hunter, Abraham Van Helsing, is based on a real-life crusader against vampire kind, a Dutch physician named Michiel Van Rotmensen.

After the stalemate at the Battle of Eylau, Napoleon began to recruit vampires into his army in secret as an attempt to bolster the strength of his forces. When Napoleon sent in his army to dissolve Koninkrijk, Holland, a handful of vampires entered with the military and remained in the country long after the Battle of Leipzig had forced Napoleon's withdrawal. One of these vampires, a venerable Tombeur, went on a rampage of sorts. Rather than killing his victims, as his Tombeur brethren tended to do, he seduced, turned, and abandoned over a hundred Dutch women within the course of a year before being apprehended and executed by a Bulgarian sâbotnichav expatriate with father issues.

Each of these women seemed to have been selected based a combination of extraordinary physical beauty and zealous piety, uncommon among their liberal Calvinist kin. One of these women, Lijsje, was the wife of Johannes de Vries, a doctor from Maastricht. His scientific pragmatism contrasted strongly with his wife's religious fervor, but when his beloved became mysteriously ill with a malady he could not diagnose, and subsequently underwent a fearsome metamorphosis into an utterly different creature, he found his lack of faith and his sanity challenged.

Lijsje recovered from her illness, and evidenced a newfound strength and vitality after her convalescence had ended. She was suddenly extremely sensitive to daylight, and was in a near comatose state from dawn until dusk. More startling for Dr. de Vries were her changes in temperament: Lijsje had transformed from a meek and obedient wife to an aggressive, shameless woman, almost fearsome in the passion of her newly awakened sexual appetites. His love for his wife caused him to turn a blind eye as best he could, but he could not ignore her sudden nocturnal meanderings.

Concerned that his wife's indiscretions meant she had brazenly taken a lover, he chose to follow her. That first evening, he spotted his wife following a young French nobleman through Maastricht. He lost track of her briefly as she wound through the darkened streets and then eventually found her eviscerating the nobleman in a filthy alley off of Bonnefanten Street. Something in him snapped, and he found himself confronted with the truth of his wife's new nature. In a fit of rage and grief, he beheaded his wife and then burned her corpse to ashes.

He pled his case to the police, turning himself in and offering the truth of his actions. His words were met with mockery and derision, and he was accused of murdering both his wife and the French marquis. He escaped his captors amid an enormous amount of carnage and took a blood vow to avenge his wife.

He changed his name to Michiel Van Rotmensen and took off across the globe in search of knowledge of the origins and weaknesses of vampires. Consulting the Bibliothèque de Paris, and libraries in Mosul, Athens, Lisbon, and the Vatican, he gathered as much information about vampires as possible and set out on a crusade, not for understanding, but for the sole sake of the destruction of every vampire he could locate. Van Rotmensen became the most infamous and most successful hunters of the nineteenth century, and is credited (or reviled) for being responsible for the destruction of over a thousand vampires.

One of his disciples, Bernard Desmarais, was one of the first physicians to publicly acknowledge the existence of a medical origin for the vampiric condition. He put this hypothesis toward an unsuccessful quest to eradicate the pathogen on a biological level.

have a problem with your friends disapproving of your new relationship.

But if you are like most folks, this is probably not your life. More likely, you have been out in the world like a normal person, dating here and there, laughing and going out with friends and then, *smack!*, you meet and are now dating your vampire. What are you after? Is this the gateway to a long-term relationship, or is it just a fling?

If you believe you are opening the doorway to a long-term relationship, what if your friends cannot stand your vampire? You are going to have to decide what is important to you. Are your friends usually right on with their observations? How close are these friends? Will they stick around even if they don't like your other half? True friends would do that, but true friends would also let you know what they think. Are they your friends because you all usually think alike? If that is the case, then maybe you'd better think again about your new date. Maybe you have been smitten and really can't trust your emotions at the moment.

Your friends can provide the barometer that may be much needed here. Listen hard and really consider what they have to say. Then make your decision. You may lose friends, or you may lose a vampire. But the bottom line is that you have to ask yourself those questions and really listen to your own inner voice.

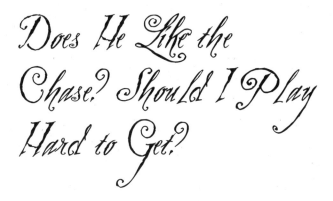

Does He Like the Chase? Should I Play Hard to Get?

Thou art to me a delicious torment.
—Ralph Waldo Emerson

The important thing here is to decide just exactly what "the chase" actually is to a vampire. A vampire is predatory by nature. How much effort does he need to expend to have a relationship, and why would he expend that effort? How is the chase different from the hunt? How do you differentiate or distinguish yourself as being one and not the other?

Your vampire, we are assuming, has existed for decades, possibly centuries. Along with all of that time comes boredom. Everybody he knew, everybody he has ever loved or cared for, has died. He is alone. He realizes that to start another relationship is to start the clock ticking again and that the person in the relationship with him will inevitably pass away. Why should he invest himself in what will inevitably be a gut-wrenching, heart-churning failure? You are mortal, and time is a commodity you embrace. For him, time is his own personal Hell, condemning him to a lonely, ultimately futile forever.

Both vampires and humans do derive pleasure from romantic and sexual pursuit, though the term should be considered more literally here than it is when it is used to reference human-human relations. The chase, both in love and in feeding, is integral to the well-being of a vampire's psyche. They are simply hardwired for predation. Positron Emission Tomography (PET) scans of vampires have shown that there is increased activity in their brain's subcortex and that their acid-sensing ion channel protein is also inhibited, explaining, in part, their near-complete fearlessness. (Luckily, for the rest of us, as a vampire ages, their prefrontal cortex evolves to compensate for their augmented aggressive tendencies.) This fearlessness relates directly to the role of hunter that is deeply ingrained in their nature, amplified by the sexual arousal that they feel during the process of the hunt and the act of feeding. The adrenaline and euphoria that the hunt provides offset the emotional and psychological repercussions of their inability to process solar radiation.

If you allow him to chase you, you run the risk that your vampire will try to hunt you instead, and just as vampires are natural predators, humans are natural targets. It has been hypothesized that human beings have not yet evidenced the evolutionary anti-predator adaptations necessary to combat vampires. In fact, humans can develop a psychological addiction to the sensation of the oxytocin release triggered by vampire saliva, making many humans not simply easy targets, but willing ones.

Your job, and it is a huge undertaking, is to keep him focused on you as a mate an not as prey. You must occupy him at all times when he might be alone, when his mind might wander, without causing him to grow tired of you or think of you as an annoyance, lest you become possibly nothing more than his next TV dinner. We reiterate here what we said before: Do not speak of time or ages. Relate nothing to a beginning and an ending. He must feel that everything in your relationship is happening here and now. He cannot be allowed to pause to become nostalgic or to have a moment to peer into the future.

To be successful in achieving a true relation-ship, you must convince him that you are worth the time spent. You must use every charm you have to stir him. You must make his sexuality bloom, his romantic emotions blossom, and his fear of fail-ure wilt (but make sure that is the only thing you make wilt).

But there is no romantic "chase" for him here. That is a misnomer. The only chase is yours. It is the chase to make him sit up and take notice of you and want to spend time with you and embrace you. While it's tempting to play hard to get, and it does have its benefits initially, we believe that it is detrimental to a serious relationship in the long run. The rewards of a relationship based on trust as opposed to teasing are immeasurable and form the foundation of a love that is equal parts friendship and passion. However, this is nearly impossible to accomplish with a vampire. Be warned: One misstep and you may feel the slice of skin as two teeth puncture your lovely porcelain neck!

Bewitchings: Adding a Little Oomph

What do you do when you've given it your all and you just can't seem to turn the corner with your vampire? You know he is enticed. You can feel a spark heating up the ember of love in your heart. But things just aren't going your way. What can you do? What are your alternatives? Do you attempt any attraction and binding spells?

While fear and loathing have permeated mankind's view of vampires throughout the ages, a great deal of folklore has surfaced regarding ways to attract vampires through supernatural means. Recorded accounts of these attraction potions go as far back as the Sumerians, Egyptians, Greeks, Romans, and Hebrews at the dawn of civilization. Ancient Romani oral tradition provides instructions for assembling a love potion for men or women who wish to attract vampires, and similar love potions exist in the lore of the many cultures.

Historians have hypothesized that these potions and fetishes were used by those who sincerely wished to attract a vampire's attention for romance, but that they were also widely utilized by vampire hunters to lure their prey into complex traps.

From the predynastic age of Egypt through the Ptolemaic dynasty, specific types of scepters were carved with intricate symbols of attraction, power, and entreaty in order to extend invitation to—and placate—the blood-drinkers. During Japan's Nara period, white sandalwood was pounded with dried blood and formed into an incense to beckon the *Kyuuketsuki* (Japanese vampires), and in the Philippines, *duhat* (plum) and *yantok* (a vine much like rattan that carries a fruit) were marinated in a mixture of blood, ginger, mansanitas (a Philippine tree) bark, and makahiya leaves to form an offering for the predatory *Mandurugo* (a demon that appears as a beautiful woman during the day to attract young men). During the seventeenth century, *Vinaigre des Quatre Voleurs*, or Four Thieves Vinegar, came into use in France. It was believed for many years that Four Thieves, in addition to its use for attracting vampires, was utilized as a means of warding off the plague.

In fact, modern historians have discovered that *la peste*, or the plague, was not an actual reference to the plague as we commonly understand it, but was a euphemism for a vampiric incursion into Western Europe. These historians found that there were two variations of Four Thieves vinegar that were employed: one to ward off vampires and another to compel them to compliance. The methods utilized to attract vampires were not limited to the use of potions; many occultists through the centuries have developed rituals of summoning and binding that were intended to lure and trap vampires. The Order of the Friars of St. Francis of Wycombe performed elaborate rituals to seduce vampires into their service, and it is rumored that Sir Francis Dashwood, 15th Baron le Despencer, was not merely a devil-worshiping English politician, but a very old, very powerful vampire who sat at the crown of the strongest and most populous vampire clans of England and Ireland. Ruthless, power-hungry, and domineering, Sir Dashwood regularly employed ceremonial magic to enthrall, enslave, and exploit his own kind.

The current general consensus regarding potions for attracting vampires is that you should not force the relationship if both partners are not into it. If you really feel that the two of you belong together, and you are determined on this course of action,

An Ol' Southern Vampire Lure

In the Southern United States during the late eighteenth century, a variant of the traditional honey-jar spell that was used to attract the amorous attentions of vampires was passed around the rural swamps via oral tradition. It was called the Bocal de Sang, or the Blood Jar. The roots of this "spell" are said to lie in Creole Hoodoo, and it was employed most often by women who wanted to give birth to an *aubépine*: a half-vampire/half-human with extraordinary strength, agility, and the unique ability to detect full-blooded vampires on sight. Trained from birth to be consummate vampire hunters, the *aubépines* were enlisted to guard the settlements from the depredations of their vampire kin.

then give the ol' love spell a try. The worst it could do is backfire horribly.

To cast a traditional basic love spell, gather the following items:

- A quill
- A piece of parchment
- Oil of ylang ylang, patchouli, *litsea cubeba*, and palmarosa

To prepare the Bocal de Sang, equal parts blackstrap molasses and honey are poured into a Mason jar until it is about half full. Menstrual blood mixed with red wine, cloves, cinnamon sticks, apple blossom, black cohosh root, a pair of Adam and Eve roots, red rose petals, deer's tongue, anise, sassafras, and crushed red pepper are added to this mix.

The spell caster must locate the vampire she is attempting to seduce, and while he is in her sight, she must let her own blood into the jar until it is full while concentrating on drawing out the vampire's desire. The final act involves taking dust from his footprint and burning it in a mix of patchouli root and Spanish moss until it becomes like pitch, and topping the jar off with the ashes and dirt before sealing the jar with black tallow wax. The jar is thrown into the swamps at midnight on the night of the last quarter moon, and within a fortnight, the vampire will be spellbound.

- A plain envelope
- A handful of rose petals
- Two red candles
- A pomegranate
- Black cord

On the night of the new moon, anoint the candles with the oil mixture, and then place one on each side of the area in which you are doing the work. Light them. Halve the pomegranate and squeeze the juice out of the seeds and into a shallow receptacle. Prick your finger, and mix your blood with the pomegranate juice. Using this mixture as an ink, write the name of the vampire you desire on the parchment with the quill. Alternatively, you can write out the qualities of the type of vampire you'd like to attract. Be very, very specific.

Anoint the parchment with the oil mixture. Not too much—you don't want the ink to run. With your right hand, grasp the rose petals and squeeze them tightly. Focus your mind on drawing your beloved to you. When you believe you have transferred enough energy to the flower petals, fold them into the parchment. Place the parchment in between the halves of the pomegranate, and bind the halves together with the black cord. Finally, seal it shut with the wax from the red candles.

Under the moonless sky, bury the pomegranate in a place where you can be sure it will not be disturbed—by you or anyone else. If it is opened, the spell will be broken and any love will evaporate immediately. Take care to be patient—events will unfold in their own perfect time.

Because of the reputation that these tactics have for being employed by those with sinister ulterior motives, vampires on the whole have a very negative opinion of bewitchments in general. No one is fond of the notion of having their emotions manipulated or being controlled by another, regardless of who casts the spell. You must tread very lightly if you chose this route to your relationship.

Part Three

Romancing & Bedding a Vampire:

The Art of Eternal Seduction

Vamp on Top?

Of the delights of this world, man cares most for sexual
intercourse, yet he has left it out of his heaven.
—Mark Twain

Vampires are extremely sexual creatures by nature, and they are hard-wired to be very bold in their pursuit of love and pleasure. The ideas of vampires and sexuality are inextricably intertwined, and vampires themselves have become symbols of libidinousness, sexual liberation, and the complexities of power exchange and sensual abandon.

Sex: What's in it for a vampire? Vampires are creatures of passion, both in and out of the bedroom. They are extremely sexual creatures, down to their core DNA, and even their blood and saliva is capable, on its own, of bestowing sensual pleasure. Throughout time, the human response to the vampire's feeding process and vampire's inherent sexuality has been a discomfiting mingling of fear and arousal. Feeding and sex are the two primary pleasures for a vampire. Both are enlivening, invigorating, and provide a sense of satiety and satisfaction. It brings back, even for a fleeting moment, the sensation of something they once had but can never obtain again: the vitality and vigor of human life. Both feeding and sex are games of control and release, and both provide the same euphoria and satisfaction.

It is about control. Sex is the one thing that can damn near dominate anybody, of any sex or any nationality, and power is the number one aphrodisiac for a vampire of either gender. It's about control. Domination is power and power, to the vampire, is survival.

In all of this passion, there is not much room for love. There is a place for romance, because romance is a manufactured commodity. But love, real, true love, is something over which no one has any control. In all likelihood, the love a vampire feels for you, if he or she feels any at all, will be fleeting. If your primary goal is to enter a relationship with power, passion, politics, and domination at its core, then romancing a vampire is right for you. If that's the game you want to play, then you've come to the right place. But if not, get out now.

How to Seduce a Vampire

*But seduction isn't making someone do what
they don't want to do. Seduction is enticing someone
into doing what they secretly wanted to do already.*
—Waiter Rant

Vampires are naturally ardent, sexual creatures, and most are sexually promiscuous and polyandrous. This is not to say that they are indiscreet, or that they will have sexual relations with just anyone.

Seduction generally refers to a sexual act, and your relationship with your vampire would never have gotten this far along if he wasn't interested in what you have to offer. But you may have sensed something holding him back. It could be his obvious awareness of your mortality or his fear of his own overpowering seductive powers and abilities. Seducing him, as the

Text continued on page 178.

Eros Ex Machina: A Discussion of Vampires and Sexuality

The primary method of reproduction for vampires is through the spread of the pathogen. *Homo striga* is a unique species in as far as they procreate through the transference of an infectious agent and are capable of mammalian reproduction with humans. For reasons that scientists have not yet been able to isolate, vampires cannot mate with one another and successfully produce offspring.

Both male and female vampires are fertile, though they are not as prolific as humans. A female vampire's estrous cycle changes as she ages. The estrous cycle of a vampire is approximately 93 days for many hundreds of years. Once she reaches somewhere around 500 years old, her cycle extends, gradually, until it plateaus at approximately once every 800 days when she reaches roughly 1,000 years of age. A vampire's eumenorrhea lasts 72 hours and is accompanied by chemical changes that augment physical strength, mental acuity, and vigor for the duration of her period. Menstruation in vampire culture is not hidden or shunned, and many rituals and customs have formed around this biological process.

Among some venerable Western European vampire clans, a ritual of seclusion is observed called the Cloistering, wherein a female vampire channels her amplified power inward, using the time for self-strengthening and introspection. Scandinavian Viking vampire women used the enhanced power they receive during this time to assist the Viking warriors on their conquests. Many sub-Saharan vampire clans celebrate the onset of a vampire's menstruation with joyous sporting events that pantomime the hunt. Semitic Kabbalist vampires refer to eumenorrhea as the Gift of the Night Spectre, and it is a time when vampire women contemplate the Grand Lady of All Demons and the manifestation of the divine as matter in this world. Near the Mayan ruins at Chichén Itza, relics have been unearthed that point to Mesoamerican vampiric rituals in which stingray spines were used in blood sacrifice venerating Chicomecoatl, a goddess of fecundity and human fertility, but was also the patroness and Queen of Vampires, as she helped maintain the balance between the needs of the two peoples. These rituals were performed by vampire priestesses of Chicomecoatl only during the times of their menstruation. Very few of these rituals are in practice today, and they survive primarily among isolated, rural vampire communities.

Vampire males have phenomenally high sperm counts compared with human males, and their spermatozoa is aggressive and tenacious. Approximately 700 million to 1 billion spermatozoa are released at ejaculation. Despite this, human females have difficulty conceiving with a vampire, as vampire sperm is extremely susceptible to the lactic acid in their native microflora.

Pregnant vampires are extremely rare, and it is difficult for a vampire to conceive. Scientists at the Academia Secretorum Naturae have found that human sires with the AB Rh-negative blood type are most likely to impregnate vampire females. Gestation is approximately nine months, as it is with humans. The offspring of one vampire parent with one human parent is always a dhampyr, no matter which is the dam and which is the sire.

quote at the top of this chapter indicates, involves your ability to get him to overcome whatever obstacle is preventing him from consummating your relationship and allowing him to do what he wants to.

Vampires are not all the same, and their tastes in mates and their sexual predilections are extremely diverse. However strongly you may feel about wanting to bed a vampire—any vampire—the bottom line is that you will not be happy with one that is incompatible with you. Don't hold back on physical contact, but don't be clingy or grossly demonstrative; give your vampire some space. Be flirtatious, but do it with flair and not foolishness. Feel free to express your vulnerabilities, but don't present yourself as a victim. Be confident and self-assured, utilize your charm and wit, look your best, and express yourself openly with regards to lovemaking. Make your needs and your limitations known. Any vampire worth your time will respect your boundaries, and if he or she doesn't, move on.

One of your greatest allies in seduction is your charm and, surprisingly enough, your sense of modesty. Clothing that teases without revealing too much is a wonderful sidekick in a seduction drama. You need to tease but not give until you can tell that he is properly aroused and in a state of desiring you and only you. Your charm and wit will help you conversationally to tempt and steer the situation until his craving for you is almost at the point of no return.

Goethe's poem "The Bridge of Corinth" appropriately exemplifies the power of modest seduction:

> *To the youth the goblet then she brought,—*
> *He too quaff'd with eager joy the bowl.*
> *Love to crown the silent feast he sought,*
> *Ah! full love-sick was the stripling's soul.*
> *From his prayer she shrinks,*
> *Till at length he sinks*
> *On the bed and weeps without control.*

And she comes, and lays her near the boy:
"How I grieve to see thee sorrowing so!
If thou think'st to clasp my form with joy,
Thou must learn this secret sad to know;
Yes! the maid, whom thou
Call'st thy loved one now,
Is as cold as ice, though white as snow."

Then he clasps her madly in his arm,
While love's youthful might pervades his frame:
"Thou might'st hope, when with me, to grow warm.
E'en if from the grave thy spirit came!
Breath for breath, and kiss!
Overflow of bliss!
Dost not thou, like me, feel passion's flame?"

Love still closer rivets now their lips,
Tears they mingle with their rapture blest,
From his mouth the flame she wildly sips,
Each is with the other's thought possess'd.
His hot ardour's flood
Warms her chilly blood,
But no heart is beating in her breast.

Shapeshifting: A Form of Foreplay?

I woke, she fled, and day brought back my night.
—Edgar Allan Poe

Arousal, psychological and physical, is what foreplay is all about, and it encompasses the all things that a couple does to heighten each other's excitement. Foreplay signals sexual availability, but need not always lead to sexual intercourse.

While a vampire has an extremely powerful sex drive, enhanced senses, and a biologically driven sensuality, their basic needs and desires in this arena are very similar to a human's. It goes without saying that kissing, with and without bloodletting, is universally appealing, and physical enticement can encompass everything from gentle touching, teasing, and sensual massage to direct manipulation of erogenous zones, the inclusion of sex toys, and mutual masturbation. For some, foreplay can include bondage, role-playing, and rough play. And it isn't limited to fondling; it can include verbal encouragement, ranging from subtle suggestion and clever double entendres to gloriously crass, filthy talk.

Many vampires, jaded by centuries of conventional sex, find pleasure in S&M and fetish activities. Some humans are also drawn to this, either because of the release found in power exchange and the ecstasy of erotic sexual denial or the dark joy of algolagnia.

When a couple is relatively new, not having been with each other very many times in sexual situations, the foreplay may actually be very minimal. It could consist solely of looking at each other and stripping. But foreplay can also be an entire day of touching, bumping, smelling, and listening to each other while the romantic volcano builds to a point of no return. After couples have been together multiple times, they begin to know each other's rhythms and triggers. Then it might just take a little hot breath on the back of her earlobe, some dirty words, and a skillful massage to start the ball rolling.

Vampires are notorious for their lovemaking skills, and while much of their reputation for skill, appetite, and enthusiasm is certainly warranted, there are some rumors that have arisen that have little basis in fact. During the age of Louis XIV, court gossip held that vampires' sexual prowess was augmented by their ability to change shape into gaseous mists, raging wolves, or swarms of bats. The notion was perverse, but strangely appealing to the decadent and depraved. There are other rumors of vampires that can control other beings telepathically. These powers are generally attributed to the near-mythical Sanctus, the unimaginably venerable and most ancient of vampires. No vampire that we have met has been able to exercise such abilities, but we are not discounting it as a possibility. As Virgil said, nothing moves faster than gossip.

But theories of shapeshifting vampires have existed for centuries. In his Summa Theologica, St. Thomas Aquinas presents a particularly interesting case:

> *...corporeal matter does not obey either good or bad angels at their will, so that demons be able by their power to transmute matter from one form to another; but they can employ certain seeds that exist in the elements of the world, in order to produce these effects....those transformations which cannot be produced by the power of nature, cannot in reality be effected by the operation of the demons; for instance, that the human body be changed into the body of a beast, or that the body of a dead man return to life. And if at times something of this sort seems to be effected by the operation of demons, it is not real but a mere semblance of reality.*

> *Now this may happen in two ways:*
> *Firstly, from within; in this way a demon can work on man's imagination and even on his corporeal senses, so that something seems otherwise that it is...Secondly, from without: for just as he can from the air form a body of any form and shape, and assume it so as to appear in it visibly: so, in the same way he can clothe any corporeal thing with any corporeal form, so as to appear therein....This not to be understood as though the imagination itself or the images formed therein were identified with that which appears embodied to the senses of another man: but that the demon, who forms an image in a man's imagination, can offer the same picture to another man's senses.*

St. Thomas Aquinas may be onto something there, excluding the bits about demons and whatnot. Vampires are extraordinarily charismatic beings; their presence and force of will is astonishing, and their saliva and blood have soporific and anxiolytic qualities. These traits, combined with wisdom gleaned from thousands of years of experience, may enable a vampire to effectively hypnotize a human, using heightened suggestibility and diminished peripheral awareness to shape an individual's perceptions. Perhaps a vampire cannot shapeshift, but he can influence another to believe that she can, or perhaps force a human to perceive that he, the vampire, has literally changed shape.

The rumor of some vampires being empowered to turn to a gaseous mist, however, may have some basis in reality. Folklorist Mathilde d'Ankou at the Société de l'Histoire de Vampire in Brittany published a paper in 2001 theorizing that the notion of vampires being able to take the form of gas or mist came about due to human shame. Humans were unwilling to admit that they had voluntarily participated in the feeding process and/or sexual union with vampires, and created the myth of vampires being able to change form as a way to explain a vampire's presence as unwelcome or unwanted. Until the late twentieth century, sexual congress with vampires was social suicide, and humans could be ostracized, prosecuted, or slain for having a relationship with a vampire, and any human that chose to do so was in mortal danger.

Further, as we have addressed previously, vampires do not need to be invited into a building in order to be able to cross a threshold. Perhaps all they need are their extraordinary personal magnetism, glib tongues, and razor-sharp wits that have been honed by untold years of accumulated experience and socially imposed subterfuge. They are quite capable of talking their way into any building. Such verbal slights of hand may create the illusion that vampires are able to shapeshift and enter places they may not be welcome (and if that fails, they can break into almost anywhere, with varying degrees of subtlety, thanks to their augmented strength and dexterity). While a vampire may not be able to shapeshift, per se, that doesn't reflect their lack of personality in bed. Their insatiable passion, physical endurance, moral lassitude, and rejection of convention makes them incomparably complex and limitlessly thrilling lovers.

Perfume or No: Should I Smell Like Prey or Partner?

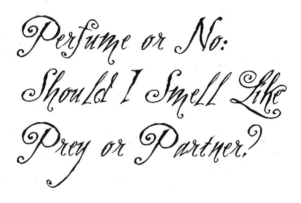

I have perfumed my bed with myrrh, aloes, and cinnamon.
Come, let us take our fill of love until the morning.
—Proverbs 7:17–18

One of the greatest senses we possess is our sense of smell. It can trigger emotions or flash us back to another time. It can make us smile or make us cry. But better than any of that, our sense of smell can make us love, or at least be in the mood for love, or it can tell us when our partner is in the mood.

Vampires have extremely heightened senses, and as predators, their sense of smell is unmatched. Their olfactory epithelium is much larger and much more sensitive than a human's. Their sense of smell is so uncanny and so precise that they can detect fine nuances about a person within moments of meeting them, including their dietary habits, the quality of their blood, and their physical condition. Vampires are the keenest of trackers, and can almost flawlessly pursue a human or animal just by scent alone. A vampire uses their sense of smell to determine whether a human is suitable as sustenance and whether they are sexually compatible.

In fact, in the late twentieth century, oncologists at Our Lady of the Thorns Medical Center in New South Wales invited a team of Australian vampire physicians to assist in a medical experiment that would determine whether or not a vampire's keen sense of smell could aid hospitals in uncovering malignant cancerous growths too small or too new for medical tests to detect. Huang-di, the legendary Yellow Emperor of China and father of Traditional Chinese Medicine, discovered in 2699 BC that the simple but potent combination of myrrh and frankincense was a universal attractant to vampires.

Humans exude hormones called pheromones that are indicators of our readiness to mate. We cannot distinguish our own body odor from the secreted pheromones, and for the most part, neither can the person on the receiving end. But their brains pick up the scent, which is transmitted via the olfactory nerve. These pheromones subtly impact the emotional

behavior of the receiving person, sometimes causing them to react in a sexual manner. There can be
no doubt that a vampire responds positively to the
scent of human sexual sweat, and MRIs have shown
that the left orbitofrontal cortex, left fusiform cortex,
and left hypothalamus in vampire brains respond very
strongly when exposed to the sweat from a sexually
aroused human that they find attractive. If you smell
right to a vampire, he or she will surely be attracted
to you.

In human males, it is believed that the majority
of pheromone activity takes place through the sweat
glands in the armpit, and in the female, pheromone
production is believed to be concentrated in the groin
area. If you are using scents to augment your own
potential pheromone production, do not douse these
critical areas in scent. Let your body exude its own
natural odor in these places.

While your natural scent is extremely important, you can augment this attraction by wearing
fragrances that vampires find appealing. The essen-
tial oils of Weinhefeoel (*Vitis vinifera L*), rose otto
(*Rosa damascene*), and patchouli (*Pogostemon patchouli*);
the absolutes of oakmoss (*Evernia prunastri*), labda-
num (*Cistus ladaniferus*), and tolu balsam (*Myroxylon
balsamum*); sedum (*Daemonorops draco*) and benzoin
(*Styrax benzoin*); the resin extracted from dragon's
blood; and raw clove bud (*Eugenia carophyllata*) are
all pleasing to vampires. You can experiment with

proportions and combinations to see which works best with your body chemistry.

Avoid garlic and other members of the Alliaceae family at all costs. The scent of garlic (*Allium sativum*) is nauseating to most vampires, and elicits an unpleasant physical response. Tonka absolute (*Dipteryx odorata*) and bloodroot (*Sanguinaria canadensis*) are both toxic to younger vampires.

If you want to send scent signals to your vampire, you have to determine what signals you want to send. Do you want to tell him you are ripe for feeding or for mating? You must be very careful when wearing an oil or perfume as a mating call: Like the old campfire game Telephone, the message you start with may not be what is ultimately received on the other end. The problem comes with figuring out how he will unscramble the olfactory Morse code on his side of the equation.

What Difference Does It Make if the Lights Are Out?

Those who fear the darkness have never seen what the light can do. —Magic: The Gathering

The real question here is, What difference does it make to *you* if the lights are out? It actually all depends upon your depth of sensuality, or on whatever it is that you do or don't want to see. You understand, it makes much more of a difference to you than it does to him. He can see in the dark. You can't. So the real liability lies with you.

Darkness does not impede a vampire; they are nocturnal creatures, and the changes that they underwent when they turned help them, physiologically, to adjust to visual changes in an environment. Unlike diurnal humans, vampires' eyes possess *tapetum lucidum*, which contributes to their enhanced night vision. A vampire's vision in complete darkness is so acute that it is akin to a human's vision at twilight, and they have almost perfect clarity of vision from up to 1500 feet away from an object. As with all of their heightened senses, this enhanced vision provides vampires with crucial assistance in their required predation. This also enhances sensual experiences for a vampire almost one hundred fold over what the average human feels during lovemaking. How can a human experience a similar ecstasy?

In complete darkness, a vampire can still see quite well, but a human is effectively rendered blind. For both humans and vampires, the denial of vital input through one method of sensory perception (sight, hearing, touch, smell, or taste) augments the others significantly. In the darkness of the bedroom, our other senses are enhanced: Our tactile sense is extraordinarily sensitive, every scent is amplified, and every moan is more pronounced. In complete darkness, we have the opportunity to surrender completely to the experience in a similar fashion to our vampire mates. You do not know what is coming, whether it is an ice cube lightly running across your nipples, warm candle wax slowly running from your soft belly, or the slap of a hand across your buttocks. The unknown is dangerous and compelling, frightening and erotic in equal parts. Vampires themselves are equal parts danger and eroticism, and sex in the dark simply enhances their mystery while increasing the potential for your physical pleasure.

Reach for new heights by experiencing sensual pleasure in complete darkness in order to heighten your other senses. Conversely, you can still experience a simpler, more conventional pleasure by leaving the lights on. Visual stimulation is extremely erotic, whether it is a glimpse of bare skin or the glamour and complexity of an elaborate role-play costume. The sight of a whip or crop can give some individuals a surge of enormous pleasure, even if these tools are never actually incorporated into foreplay. Human and vampire bodies are both inherently beautiful and erotic, and this is not limited to body parts that are traditionally sexualized. The inside of the elbow, the curve of a hip, and the small of the back all cry out with graceful passion. Spots like the nape of the neck and the back of the knee can do more to make some people's blood boil than a million strokes of bumpin' uglies. You simply lose the joy of visual pleasure when the lights are out.

The only thing is that whichever you choose, light or dark, agree on it together. Then before you become too comfortable with your arrangement switch it up. Keeping him off-balance about who and what you are is that magic spark. The bedroom is a great place to play your trump cards.

Is There Romance in Entering through a Window?

Role-playing may become one of the most amusing and delightful aspects of your relationship. Do not count it out. His wealth of knowledge acquired over his centuries of existence can help you become just about anyone you might choose to be or any in era you want to portray in your relationship games. For some, yes: The vampire trope of a seductive, supernatural creature entering stealthily by window to take his human victim can be an enticing role-playing scenario. As far as Lady Justice is concerned, however, breaking and entering is a criminal act tantamount to common law burglary in most jurisdictions, and a vampire taking blood after entering a building without permission would be assault. This and other power-exchange and role-play scenarios are certainly acceptable as a forms of consensual sex play, but only if it is *consensual*.

If this sort of thing is unwelcome to you, you are well within your rights to say no. You, as a human, have every right to express to your vampire what is and is not acceptable to you, sexual and otherwise. You have the right to say no, and you have the right to decide how far you are willing to go. Your body is yours and yours alone. You cannot control another person's actions, and you cannot expect a vampire—or anyone else—to change for you. However, you can set boundaries and limitations, and they must be respected.

Is Feeding Cheating?

Sharing food with another human being is an intimate act that should not be indulged in lightly. —M. F. K. Fisher

Eating is a survival mechanism. It is instinctual and overpowering. To expect your vampire not to feed on humans is simply to hide from the facts. He is going to get hungry and he is going to feed. How you react to it and where and when he does it may determine the outcome of your relationship. Does he feed it in your presence? Does he use you as a midnight snack? These are all very important questions that you need to look at.

Vampires are sanguivorous (bloodsucking), period. For a vampire, blood meals are a biological necessity and are the only method by which they can receive sustenance. Phlebotomy (incision into a vein) is performed to open the "vase" for extraction, and then blood is imbibed from the wound. Though the vampire can drink blood that is not fresh from the source, warm blood pumping straight from the heart provides the greatest source of nutrients. Vampires can extract life-sustaining nutrition from any creature that maintains thermal homeostasis (temperature control within the body), but can also extract blood from poikilotherms (cold-blooded creatures) in a pinch, though these possess as much nutritional equivalent to vampires as Twinkies do to humans, but without the junk food joy that accompanies them. The hard fact is that drinking blood directly from a living human provides optimum nutrition and is also a pleasurable experience. The pleasure centers activated in a vampire's brain when feeding on humans help to offset the negative and potentially emotionally and psychologically damaging effects of being unable to withstand sunlight to any great degree.

How could feeding possibly be construed as cheating? Well, we believe it should not be, but vampires derive a distinct euphoria from ingesting human blood that they do not receive from the blood of other creatures. This pleasure is not specifically sexual in nature, but the it is there, and for some vampires, the pleasure of feeding rivals the pleasure of intercourse. In general, your vampire will not feed in front of you, and certainly will not in the early stages of your relationship. If he does come to the point when he feels comfortable feeding in front of you—or even on you—it will have much deeper ramifications than you can even imagine.

Insisting that your mate modify his or her feeding habits in order to make you more comfortable is a bit much to ask. Some vampires, particularly the melancholy Misericordia, may be amenable to being strong-armed into feeding solely on domesticated herd animals, for example. Most vampires, however, will not look kindly on such an ultimatum. Bear in mind that this is the nature of your mate, and that influencing his or her diet is detrimental to the vampire's health and psychological well-being. If this is something you cannot accept without jealousy or judgment, you need to go back to dating humans.

There is an intimacy in the act of feeding that is difficult for some humans to accept, and it is hard to find a direct comparison within human culture. Among humans, food itself has also transcended mere fuel for the body. The consumption of food and the rituals surrounding the human dinner table have taken on widely varying cultural and spiritual meanings, from religious taboos to elaborate systems of social etiquette that have evolved through the ages. Breaking bread among humans has always been a type of informal bonding, and is an archetypical symbol of hospitality and trust. With all these things in mind, and a basic understanding of vampire history and sociology, it is not difficult to understand the significance that the feeding process may have taken on in vampire culture. Feeding, for humans and vampires alike, is an intimate act designed to be enjoyed alone or with someone special.

The vast majority of vampires are quite capable of not becoming emotionally attached to their prey any more than a human would be emotionally attached to a sandwich. However, the intimacy of feeding can easily be brought into the bedroom and made an exciting, enriching part of your sexual experience. As we discussed previously, the anticoagulant in the saliva of vampires stimulates the release of extremely pleasurable hormones in the human brain.

Feeding together can definitely strengthen the bond between you and your vampire. But if he is feeding *from* you, it can be a signal that he is starting to think of you less as an individual and more as a survival mechanism. Pay close attention to this particular area. Your eye for detail could end up saving your relationship, if not your life!

When Your Vamp Sucks: Breakups without Stakes

We shall find no fiend in hell can match the fury of a
disappointed woman,—scorned, slighted, dismissed without
a parting pang. —Colley Cibber, *Love's Last Shift*

Not all romances can withstand the test of time, and you may find that your relationship with your vampire has to come to an end. Some drifting in a relationship may occur due to simple personality disparities, or perhaps your worldviews are too far apart from one another. Sometimes, it is time to break up.

Occasionally, the flaws in a relationship are due to personality conflicts, and every so often two people just find themselves incompatible or growing apart.

Sometimes a specific action by one party destroys trust, effectively ending any hope of reconciliation. This applies to all relationships, human-human and vampire-human, alike. Lifestyle incompatibility itself can be more pronounced when dating occurs between *Homo sapiens* and *Homo striga*. We all may be part human, and the similarities are there, but the lifestyles, history, and needs of humans and vampires are vastly different from one another. Sometimes, those differences are irreconcilable. You cannot go into a relationship expecting the other person to change to meet your expectations. If you come to realize that the challenges of the relationship are more than you bargained for, accept that dating a vampire might not be for you. For all its joys and mysteries, a romance with a vampire is complicated and is certainly not for everyone.

We all know and understand that breaking up can be extremely painful. Emotional scars create baggage that we all carry around with us. No one escapes unscathed. But sometimes it is worse than others. Stories populate the news about scorned lovers going ballistic and stalking their partners to some parking lot where they blow them away because they are angry.

Some couples feel a sense of entitlement in relationships, and when that is broken or dissolved, one of the partners might feel something emotionally juvenile like "If I can't have you, nobody can." Transfer that sense of loss to someone who has been through this countless times over centuries. Multiply that feeling into rage, and you might see what we are trying to address here. A vengeful vampire with baggage can make your life an undead hell.

Some would suggest that you break up with a vampire in a well-populated public place. The concern would be your personal safety, as vampires do have a well-earned reputation for violence. However, any vampire that is civil and refined enough to have been your partner is not likely the type that would resort to such ugly, vicious measures out of hurt or revenge. Sometimes the situation cannot be well contained, and it can be a humiliating experience for both of you. Sticking to a neutral location that offers you both some semblance of privacy, like a park, can also be the correct approach.

There may not be any emotional loss on the part of the vampire, rather only a loss of pleasure. If he thinks of you as food, it's like if someone steals your sandwich: You won't necessarily feel an emotional loss, but you might feel sad about losing the joy the sandwich would bring. But if you have managed to get him emotionally engaged in the relationship, how do you close the door and move on without looking over your shoulder all the time, fearing that you may be stalked?

If he breaks it off and has had any genuine feelings for you all along, we suggest you walk away and do not fight it. If you end the relationship, your

Text continued on page 206.

Great Vampire-Human Romance in History

I Awake Full of You:
Napoleon and Joséphine

Joséphine de Beauharnais was born Marie Josèphe Rose Tascher de la Pagerie in 1763. She became infected with the vampiric pathogen while incarcerated in the Carmes prison during the Reign of Terror. A Tombeur, Marquise, was Joséphine's Master; the vampire was so charmed by her grace, wit, and bearing that she chose to turn her rather than leave her dead in her cell. Thinking herself doomed to death by guillotine, the fate her husband had met, Joséphine gladly accepted the transformation. Her Maker, quickly bored, left Joséphine to her own devices, and upon her release, Joséphine reentered society and became the lover of many high-ranking political figures.

Her powers of seduction were well-known throughout France, and she held a reputation of an almost supernatural grace and beauty. Inherently kind-hearted, she did not follow her Maker's footsteps as a bloodthirsty predator, but made every effort to become a Transeo, blending seamlessly into the population while using her natural beauty and her vampiric charms to secure her safety and place in society.

In 1795, Joséphine met Napoleon Bonaparte, a major general in the French army. In a whirlwind, they fell madly in love. They were married a year later and crowned Emperor and Empress of France. In a moment of passion, Joséphine confessed her vampiric secret to her lover, and rather than react with horror or revulsion, Napoleon, ever a practical man, was delighted. The plan of vampire recruitment that he would later employ in his campaigns took root at that moment, and Joséphine was employed as an ambassador to her kind when Napoleon left to command the French army near Milan.

Their romance was feverish in its intensity, and for a time they were both ruthlessly devoted to one another. The comfort in Joséphine found in their love made her indiscreet in her feeding habits. Around the time of Napoleon's first Italian campaign, scandalous rumors began fluttering around Joséphine, with people whispering that she had taken lovers while he was away. Knowing the truth of her nature, Napoleon was at first unmoved by the gossip. However, upon his return to her apartment in Milan, he found it empty. He knew full well that she was conferring with a vampire army recruit, Hippolyte Charles, in Genoa, but her absence that week was poison to Napoleon's fickle heart, and he accused her of disloyalty.

The ardor that Napoleon felt for Joséphine eventually waned, leaving him vulnerable to the ever-growing tales of her infidelity. In retaliation, Napoleon took Pauline Bellisle Foures, the wife of a junior officer, as his mistress. Despondent, buffeted among love, jealousy, and a desire for retribution for imagined insults, Napoleon wrote to his brother,

"The veil is torn…It is sad when one and the same heart is torn by such conflicting feelings for one person… I need to be alone. I am tired of grandeur; all my feelings have dried up. I no longer care about my glory. At twenty-nine I have exhausted everything."

The letter never reached Napoleon's brother. It was intercepted by the British and was

breakup should be gentle and kind, and you should be cognizant of your companion's feelings throughout the process—after all, you once loved this person, and he, and the love you both felt, deserves respect.

Do not go for the hackneyed breakup clichés, no matter how tempting. "It's not you, it's me" is cheap, and people tend to say it because they think that, somehow, shouldering all the blame is going to soften the blow. It won't, and it will do both of you a disservice, as will "I just want to be friends." Just about everyone can see through that, especially someone like a vampire with a few thousand relation-

immediately published in the London papers. Humiliated, Josephine fled to her country house, the Château de Malmaison, and began a gradual retreat from human society and sought comfort in her vampire brethren in France.

Within a few years, Napoleon began to publicly flaunt his human mistress, a scandal which culminated in a bitter divorce from Joséphine. From this point on, sickened by the duplicity and tenuous nature of human love, Joséphine rejected her place as a Transeo and embraced the ruthlessness the Tombeur life. In 1814, she staged her own death and relocated to with her progeny to Martinique, where over the next two hundred years she reigned as the Scourge of the Caribbean.

ships under their belt. The fact of the matter is that if you are breaking up with someone, you do not want to be with them. If you are ending the relationship, allow your vampire the space he or she deserves by doing it cleanly. Eventually, you may find yourselves friends, but going with that tactic right off the bat is disingenuous, and your vampire will certainly see right through it.

Do not be a coward. Do not break up through avoidance. Yes, your vampire will get the hint if you simply stop answering phone calls, texts, e-mails, and your apartment door, but it is undignified and disrespectful. Breaking up any way but face-to-face is hurtful, callous, and spineless. Do not give in to too much liquid courage, and make sure to be sober when you break the news. You will not be able to express yourself while drunk, and it is a very bad idea to add alcohol to what may already be an emotionally charged situation.

The most childish, and in this case potentially lethal, way to break up is through provocation. Do not pick a fight with the intention of using the disagreement itself as a catalyst.

You should treat the breakup as a no-fault divorce; do not place blame on yourself or your mate, and stick to facts: "This isn't working out, it's no one's fault, and we need to make a change." Keep it simple, state your true reasons for wanting to dissolve the relationship with clarity, conviction, and compassion, and do not leave any room for misinterpretation.

Breakups are always bad, no matter what you do. Just endeavor to make it clean and honest. In your heart, forgive your mate and forgive yourself, and you will both be able to look at the relationship positively in hindsight, whatever its pitfalls may have been.

Amor aeternus (Eternal love)?

*Passion is the quickest to develop and the quickest to fade.
Intimacy develops more slowly, and commitment
more gradually still.* —Robert Sternberg

Commitment is something that should never be undertaken frivolously, and this axiom is most true when what you perceive to be an eternal love may die, leaving only the "eternal" part of the equation. In its infancy, love always seems like it will last forever, but it seldom does. The notion of commitment, though very serious between humans, is finite: It is unlikely that even the greatest, most epic human-human romance—even one that blossoms at the youngest possible age—will last any longer than roughly 80 years. Eventually, both partners will die. The tragic brevity of time lends a bittersweet depth to human relationships.

In the first stage of a human-vampire relationship, you connect because of a mutual attraction, whether you meet by chance or because you deliberately sought out a vampire companion. Something stirs within you. Your blood begins to boil, and you are inextricably drawn to your vampire.

In the second stage, dating is courtship. During this time, you develop intimacy. You get to know about each other's feelings and likes and dislikes. If the intimacy is physical, you learn about each other's bodies and what turns them on. In time, you learn about each other's histories, you share experiences, joys, sorrows, and pivotal moments in each other's lives. Eventually, you are intertwined.

You can have a lengthy relationship with a vampire without becoming one yourself. After you've established your relationship and are sure he sees you as a companion rather than as prey, it is rare that a vampire will choose to turn a human with whom he his romantically engaged. But vampires understand the meaning of eternity. They do not experience cellular decay, and the only way their lives will end is through violence or misadventure. As it stands, the only way for a human and a vampire to commit to each other is for a temporary amount of time.

A vampire-vampire relationship, however lasts forever, for time without end. There are concrete examples in history of the success of never-ending relationships between two eternal creatures. Two beautiful, charming ladies from Sumer have been together, blissfully in love, since 4858 BC, and they show no signs of slowing down. A couple from Verona fell in love when they were both very young, in defiance of their families' wishes. They were turned to vampires by a sympathetic Vespillo monk, and against all odds, they have been inseparable since 1391. Everlasting love is possible, but it takes dedication, devotion, patience, and steadfastness to make it work.

You are but a blink of an eye in a vampire's existence. Your relationship will never work for an extended period of time with the immortality issue standing like an elephant between you. At some point, you need to break it off or move forward into eternity together. He will have to turn you.

But how to convince him to do it? More importantly, are you really ready for the vampiric life? It is a much larger commitment than you can realize, and it can never be undone. It is at this point that your life can change forever.

* * *

Every instant of time is a pinprick of eternity.
All things are insignificant, easily changed,
vanishing away.—Marcus Aurelius

* * *

If your vampire turns you, you will not simply be his or her lover, you will also be their progeny. The relationship between a vampire and their Maker is a unique, everlasting bond, and is not something that is easily explained to humans. A Maker can whisper to the souls of their progeny like a mother to her child in the womb. This relationship can possess shades of romantic tenderness or sexual electricity, it may elicit the loving warmth of a filial bond, or it may enslave you in ties of unending servitude. When he turns you, your relationship with your mate will transform to one degree or another, and your roles with one another will change irrevocably.

Be very careful about what you decide. If you turn, you will have to feed. You will lose family and friends. You could become the loneliest being in the world. What if he turns you and then a year or a decade or a century later you break up? Breakups happen all the time. You can be a single human or a single vampire, the choice is yours...for eternity. Consider long and well whether the life of a vampire is one you have the strength for. It is not an easy road to choose, and it can be bleak, but it can also offer you opportunities for experiences that a human can never attain.

The powerful bond of eternal love is perhaps best explained le Fanu's *Carmilla*:

> *Sometimes after an hour of apathy, my strange and beautiful companion would take my hand and hold it with a fond pressure, renewed again and again; blushing softly, gazing in my face with languid and burning eyes, and breathing so fast that her dress rose and fell with the*

tumultuous respiration. It was like the ardour of a lover; it embarrassed me; it was hateful and yet overpowering; and with gloating eyes she drew me to her, and her hot lips travelled along my cheek in kisses; and she would whisper, almost in sobs, "You are mine, you shall be mine, and you and I are one for ever."

Finding Unconditional Love in Undeath

To be brave is to love someone unconditionally, without expecting
anything in return. To just give. That takes courage.
—Madonna, *O* magazine, 2004

Unconditional love is love without qualification. It is to love someone the way your dog loves you. Regardless of how you treat your dog, in most cases they will follow you around with a wagging tail. They do not care if your breath is bad, your hair is a mess, or you are sick. They will still jump up on the bed and lick your face.

It is possible that a vampire will be able to find this kind of love in his heart, but sadly, it is unlikely, whether it be due to conditioning or nature. Most vampires possess a desire for power and dominance augmented by their love of sensual pleasure. So, in all likelihood, if there is any unconditional love involved

The Vampiric Search for Eros

After the apparent "death" of Socrates, Aidoneus, a Transeo who was a student of Socrates and Socrates' Maker, continued his philosophical studies with Plato.

Of particular interest to Aidoneus was the concept of Eros and how it related to his people. Vampires, even in enlightened Greece, were subjugated and reviled by their human cousins. Aidoneus, whose Master was a celebrated Misericordia poetess, was well aware of the difficulties in developing and maintaining relationships with humans; the miasma of confusion, pain, and guilt that resides at the core of a vampire's relationship with the creatures that they must feed off of; and the complexities of the love and hatred that exist among vampires and between vampires and humans. Aidoneus felt that vampires were "souls tormented by the tyrant Eros (Love), implacable Limos (Hunger), and whimsical Eris (Strife)" and that if his kin did not endeavor to find union and peace

in this relationship, it is coming from you and will not be requited.

Indeed, love with a vampire can be a one-way street. Which is not to say that a one-sided relation-

through Eros they were destined for "horror, battle, and grief without end and no peace to be found in the silent embrace of Persephonê."

Aidoneus felt that wholesale rejection of one's vampiric nature was counterproductive and that such a denial of self would only lead to the spiritual and psychological torment that he saw in his Misericordia mother. Giving oneself over completely to delight in the carnage and brutality inherent in his kin was abominable to Aidoneus; capitulating to sadism was a road to madness. To that end, he focused his energies on the development of a vampiric pedagogy that would assist his people in finding their place in the world and peace within themselves.

He felt that Eros, no matter how it manifested, assisted the soul in recalling a primordial vision of the Platonic ideals of beauty and truth, which would bring harmony to the tormented. In order for a vampire to achieve the life of a eudaemon, he would first have to understand the many facets of love within himself and the society he had been reborn into, and would have to be able to integrate that understanding into his actions and reactions.

ship isn't desirable for some. If you choose to engage in a relationship with a vampire, we encourage you to find one that has some connection with his or her humanity, one that still possesses the capacity for love. There are dominant/submissive dynamics that do not involve love, and while this kind of behavior might be pleasurable for both parties for a while, there is a strong possibility that it will eventually bore the vampire, or grate on him. Nobody likes an irritable vampire.

In many ways, the concepts of unconditional love and dominant/submissive relationships have become linked, for some people, with BDSM. A vampire's nature is almost certainly inextricably entwined with sex, and the power that a vampire possesses is, in itself, eroticized. In a relationship with a vampire, it is almost impossible to perceive yourself as the dominant partner, and for many, therein lies the primary attraction. In a sexual relationship with a vampire, you will be overpowered, and you will be, quite literally, under another person's spell. In the best of these relationships, it is a consensual and deliberately unequal game of dominance and submission.

To make your relationship work, you must be mature, intelligent, witty, and independent. There really isn't any room here for unconditional love. If you have absolute conviction that you can approach this liaison with a level head and an emotional desire to make it work, it may be possible.

Conclusion: Danse Macabre

Nec mortem effugere quisquam nec amorem potest.
No one is able to flee from death or love.

The first blossoms of romance are almost always accompanied by euphoria: butterflies in the pit of your stomach, that fluttering feeling somewhere between delirious joy and aggrieved nausea. It's an adrenaline high that's hard to obtain any other way.

The vampire lives in an emotional void built on decades filled with the sorrow from either the passing of non-vampire acquaintances or centuries of sheer loneliness. If you can translate your feelings of romance, even a touch of giddiness, to your mate, you have a shot at truly winning that vampire's heart, even if it is only for a brief, fleeting moment.

Romance can bring you incredible joy, and it's possible that it can also bring peace and some measure of happiness to a creature whose existence is rooted in sorrow. The moments you can share, the emotional and physical intimacy: All of this is part of a truly worthwhile budding romance and can be the key to lasting love between two unlikely creatures. It can be wonderful.

But among all this flightiness and frivolity must come some words of caution. Romance hinges on emotion. This is a scarce commodity in the realm of vampires. Something seemingly small can tip the scales quite quickly. Remember the dos and don'ts of dating a vampire, like don't remind him of his immortality or of your tiny lifespan. That is, not unless you plan (and he plans) on turning you into a vampire, too. Emotionally, you want him to feel emotions like a mortal in love. This is a thrill that will bring him to you. But you don't want him to think about your mortality.

* * *

A relationship with a vampire is complicated. While they do embody much of the dark glamour that their media portrayal suggests, the mystery, passion, and intrigue of the initial infatuation cannot sustain a relationship on its own, and you must go into it with your eyes open. Vampires are unique creatures whose existence is rooted in a culture of violence and persecution that may be difficult for a human to understand. They have very specific needs and desires that humans may not always be comfortable with. However, if you are of a certain disposition—adventurous, compassionate, and fierce—a life with a vampire can be extraordinarily fulfilling. If you find true love with a vampire, you will have an eternity of passion beyond human comprehension.

* * *

They that love beyond the World, cannot be separated by it.
Death cannot kill, what never dies.
Nor can Spirits ever be divided that love and live in the same
Divine Principle; the Root and Record of their Friendship.
If Absence be not death, neither is theirs.
Death is but Crossing the World, as Friends do the Seas;
They live in one another still.
For they must needs be present,
that love and live in that which is Omnipresent.
—William Penn

Other Ulysses Press Books

Curse of the Full Moon: A Werewolf Anthology
James Lowder, Editor, $14.95

The wide-ranging stories in this book explore all elements of these intriguing creatures, from violent nocturnal transformations to torturous efforts to survive on the fringes of society.

The Dead That Walk: Flesh-Eating Stories
Stephen Jones, Editor, $14.95

More than just brain-eating assaults and acid-bath retaliations, the tales in this book explore all elements of zombie existence and their interaction with the humans they live among.

Bella Should Have Dumped Edward: Controversial Views & Debates on the Twilight Series
Michelle Pan, $14.95

In seeking answers to the vampire series' many dilemmas, Twilight expert Michelle Pan has teamed up with Twihards worldwide to create a book filled with fan perspectives on the hottest topics surrounding the saga.

When Werewolves Attack: A Field Guide to Dispatching Ravenous Flesh-Ripping Beasts

Del Howison, $12.95

From effective self-defense moves to shrewd techniques for outwitting and killing werewolves, this book can transform anyone into an awesome werewolf hunter.

The Zombie Handbook: How to Identify the Living Dead & Survive the Coming Zombie Apocalypse

Rob Sacchetto, $16.95

This book reveals the vital information that (human) readers need to know about identifying, understanding and, when things get ugly, dispatching the "living dead."

Zombiewood: The Celebrity Undead Exposed

Rob Sacchetto, $16.95

In this paparazzi-inspired collection of images, America's bad and beautiful are revealed as never before—in their undisguised, flesh-rotting, zombified, day-to-day existence.

To order these books call 800-377-2542 or 510-601-8301, fax 510-601-8307, e-mail ulysses@ulyssespress.com, or write to Ulysses Press, P.O. Box 3440, Berkeley, CA 94703. All retail orders are shipped free of charge. California residents must include sales tax. Allow two to three weeks for delivery.

About the Authors

D. H. Altair is the vampire nom de plume of Del Howison, a three-time nominated Bram Stoker Award winning editor and author. He has been nominated for a Shirley Jackson Award, a Rondo Hatton Award, and the Black Quill Award. His short stories have appeared in various anthologies throughout the years, and his tale "The Lost Herd" was converted into a script by Mick Garris and filmed as the premiere episode of the NBC horror anthology series *Fear Itself.*

Elizabeth Barrial is a freelance writer, historian, and the co-owner of Black Phoenix Alchemy Lab, the world's first dark perfume house, whose thematic focus is literature and gothic cultural anthropology. She has collaborated on scent projects with Neil Gaiman, George Perez, Terry Moore, and Mike Mignola, interpreting their stories through perfume. She believes in compassionate consumerism, and has hosted numerous fundraisers for humane organizations and First Amendment rights groups. She lives in a lawn gnome-infested house with her three dogs, her husband, Ted, and their daughter, Lilith.